L A … S

Li… s
of
JEAN-PAUL SARTRE

DR. ANUP KUMAR CHANDA

BlueRose ONE.com
Stories Matter
NewDelhi • London

BLUEROSE PUBLISHERS
India | U.K.

For permissions requests or inquiries regarding this publication, please contact:

BLUEROSE PUBLISHERS
www.BlueRoseONE.com
info@bluerosepublishers.com
+91 8882 898 898
+4407342408967

ISBN: 978-93-5819-669-6

Cover design: Tahira
Typesetting: Tanya Raj Upadhyay

First Edition: August 2023

To my loving wife

'Dhriti'

Your hand of encouragement will always be on my shoulder.

"If you're lonely when you're alone, you're in bad company."

-- Jean-Paul Sartre

Preface

Few academicians have been as famous in their own life-time as the twentieth century French philosopher Jean-Paul Sartre (1905–80). He was much more than just a traditional academic philosopher. He was a prolific writer. He wrote highly influential works of literature, including novels, plays and essays, inflected by philosophical concerns. Alongside, he founded and co-edited the French journal Les Temps Modernes and mobilised various forms of political protest and action.

Sartre was a sensation during his time. His treatises and novels sold in millions; his plays were huge success; his public lectures were mobbed. His intellectual standing was so high that during May 1968 strikes in Paris, Sartre was arrested for civil disobedience; but the then French President Charles de Gaulle intervened and pardoned him, commenting that "you don't arrest Voltaire."

As existentialist, Sartre believed in the essential freedom of individuals, and he also believed that as free beings, people are responsible for all elements of themselves, their consciousness, and their actions. That is, with total freedom comes total responsibility. After World War II, he began to take keen interest in French political movements as well as uprise against injustice anywhere around the world. He had strong leanings to the left and was an ardent admirer of the Soviet Union, although he did not join the French Communist Party (PCF). However, after Stalin's death and following the entry of Soviet tanks into Budapest in 1956, he became highly critical of communism and wrote in Les Temps Modernes a long article, "Le Fantôme de Staline" ('Stalin's Ghost') in which he condemned both the Soviet intervention and the submission of the PCF to the dictates of Moscow. His critical analysis of Marxism paved the way to a form of "Sartrean socialism" that found its expression in his major work, Critique de la raison dialectique ('Critique of Dialectical Reason', 1960),

Despite his disillusionment with communism as was in vogue at that time in various parts of the world, Sartre still believed that Marxism was the only philosophy for the current times, but it ought to adapt itself to particular situations, rather than attempting to fit a predetermined universal mould. Marxism, in his opinion, ought to learn to recognize the existential concrete circumstances that differ from one collective whole to another and to respect individual freedom.

After Sartre's death in 1980, his standing fell, particularly, because of his many mistakes and inconsistencies, such as, his support for Stalinism in the early 1950s, for Maoism in the 1970s, his defence of civilian massacres in Algeria and at the 1972 Munich Olympics, and he gradually faded into oblivion. Another phenomenon that contributed to gradual decline in Sartre's prominence was the rise of new heroes of "post-structuralism" in the 1960s, as a result of which Sartre's work began to receive less and less academic attention in the intellectual world. Although Gilles Deleuze dedicated an article to his "master" in 1964 in the wake of Sartre's refusal of the Nobel Prize for literature, [1] Michel Foucault indignantly declared Sartre's late work was a "magnificent and pathetic attempt of a man of the nineteenth century to think the twentieth century". [2]] The reason for Foucault's critical remark is not too difficult to comprehend. Sartre seemed to personify everything that structuralists and poststructuralists like Foucault opposed. In effect, the rock star intellectual of mid-century France,

---

1 Deleuze, Gilles, "*Desert Islands and Other Texts*", 1953–1974, David Lapoujade (trans.), Los Angeles, CA: Semiotext(e), 2004.

2 Foucault, Michel, 1966 [1994], "*L'homme est-il mort?*" (interview with C. Bonnefoy), Arts et Loisirs, no. 38 (15–21 juin): 8–9. Reprinted in Dits et Écrits, Daniel Defert, François Ewald, & Jacques Lagrange (eds.), 540–544, Paris: Gallimard, 1994. 2001, Dits et Écrits, volume 1, Paris: Gallimard.

in course of time, became the "traditionalist" of the following generation.

Interestingly, however, Sartre's reputation as one of the most important thinkers and writers of the twentieth century is rising again, particularly in high academic circles in the United States, a country he detested. The centenary celebration of his birth in 2005 has provoked a flood of re-examinations of Sartre's intellectual and political legacy.

Apart from this, a substantial part of Sartre's oeuvre, such as 'Imagination' (1936) or its sequel 'The Imaginary' (1940), his massive two-volume 'Critique of Dialectical Reason' (1960), or his five-volume masterpiece on Flaubert, 'The Family Idiot' (1971–2), has remained largely under-appreciated so far. These are amongst the works of which Sartre was most proud of and their core ideas and their relevance in the present world is now gaining attention of the scholars and researchers.

In this backdrop, at a time when his contributions are being re-evaluated, it may be of interest to look in retrospect at the life of the French philosopher Jean-Paul Sartre to appreciate how he, along with his life-long companion, Simone de Beauvoir (Author of 'The Second Sex' and popularly known as the 'Mother of Feminism') faced the turbulent world of their time. Sartre was a difficult man, and on several occasions he changed his position for reasons not quite comprehensible to others; but one thing must be admitted about him – true to his philosophy of existentialism, he lived the life he wished to live.

This book is dedicated to my wife Dhriti, who is no more. She always encouraged me to write, but I didn't listen. I hope my belated compliance will make her happy, wherever she is.

I am indebted to my parents, Late Bibhuti Bhusan Chanda and Late Binapani Chanda, for their constant love, affection and support in my life, that made me what I'm today, and gave me the courage to undertake new ventures in life. I am also grateful to my daughter Dr. Sagnika Chanda for her love and inspiration that helped me to go forward in the present venture.

I also owe my gratitude to my elder brother Shri Pradip Kumar Chanda. He has been a constant source of encouragement for me without which this book would not have been possible.

Last but not the least, I would like to gratefully acknowledge the help and untiring assistance of my dear friend Shri Baidyanath Mukhopadhyay who painstakingly went through the entire manuscript and made many valuable suggestions for improvement.

And with this, I conclude what I had to say to introduce the present book. Now, let the journey begin to explore the fascinating life, death and last words of Jean-Paul Sartre, the philosopher who rocked the world of his time.

Prologue

His Last Words

"I love you very much, my dear Castor."

--- Jean-Paul Sartre

Sartre was on death bed.

Blood circulation problem had damaged his legs, arms, heart, eyes and brain. Since 20th March, 1980, his respiratory system began to suffer severe circulation problems too. He had developed pulmonary oedema and, therefore, not enough oxygen was getting into his blood. His blood circulation had also become so poor that his kidneys began to fail and his bed sores turned gangrenous.

On 14th April, 1980, when he was given a glass of water, he tried to look cheerful: *"The next time we have a drink together, it'll be at my place and it'll be whisky!"*

Simone de Beauvoir, philosopher, author of *"The Second Sex"*, icon of the modern feminism and Sartre's life time partner, insists that these were not Sartre's last words, as some authors have claimed. According to her, the following day, Sartre, no longer trying to be cheerful, asked her how they would pay for his funeral. Drifting in and out of consciousness, he took de Beauvoir's (nicknamed "Castor") wrist and said:

"I love you very much, my dear Castor"

These were his last words

Table of Contents

Chapter 1

Sartre: Glimpses of His Life

"We must act out passion before we can feel it."

— Jean-Paul Sartre

Sartre was a novelist, playwright, political activist, and exponent of Existentialism—a philosophy acclaiming the freedom of individual. He was the founder of "*Libération*", France's most powerful left-wing newspaper, and "*Les Temps Modernes*", its premier intellectual journal.

Sartre was an intellectual rock star. His treatises and novels sold in millions; his plays were huge success; his public lectures ¿were mobbed. His stature in the intellectual world was comparable to someone like Voltaire's. In fact, during May 1968 strikes in Paris, Sartre was arrested for civil disobedience; but President Charles de Gaulle intervened and pardoned him, commenting that "*you don't arrest Voltaire*."

Sartre: The Child

"I have no superego."

--- Jean-Paul Sartre

Sartre was born in Paris on June 21, 1905, to Jean-Baptiste and Anne-Marie Sartre. His mother was née Schweitzer, from a prominent, liberal Alsatian family, and through her he was related to Nobel Peace laureate Albert Schweitzer, whom he once described as "*my cousin Albert [who] was not bad at the organ*."

Sartre's father was a French naval officer, and was on duty overseas at the time of Sartre's birth. When Sartre was a little over one year of age, his father died. The result, he wrote later in his diary, was that "*I have no superego*." [3]

His mother, the young widow, returned to her parents' house. She and her son were treated there as "the children" of the family. In his autobiography, *"Les Mots"* (*"The Words",* 1964), Sartre describes his "*unnatural*" childhood as a teenage tearaway. Raised by a doting, widowed mother and a grandfather (Charles Schweitzer, uncle of Albert Schweitzer[4]) who indulged and idealized him, Sartre recalled, "*I was not taught obedience.*"

His grandfather Charles Schweitzer, a teacher of German, taught Sartre mathematics and introduced him to classical literature at a very early age. His childhood experience convinced him that people are likely to become what they pretend to be. Sartre pretended to be the boy genius his grandfather expected. He recalled learning to read at age three or four by pretending to read. Lacking any companion of his own age, he found "*friends*" exclusively in books. Reading and writing thus became his twin passions. *"It was in books that I encountered the universe."*

The memories of Sartre's childhood are recounted in several places, including his autobiography, "*Les Mots*" ('The Words'). Although his mother once commented about this work that "*Poulou*," his childhood nickname, "*didn't understand a thing*

---

[3] The superego is the ethical component of the personality and provides the moral standards by which the ego operates. The superego's criticisms, prohibitions, and inhibitions form a person's conscience, and its positive aspirations and ideals represent one's idealized self-image, or "ego ideal." (Read Sigmund Freud's 1926 Britannica essay on psychoanalysis.)

[4] Recipient of 1952 Nobel Peace Prize for his philosophy of "*Reverence for Life*", becoming the eighth Frenchman to be awarded that prize. His philosophy was expressed in many ways, but most famously in founding and sustaining the Hôpital Albert Schweitzer in Lambaréné, French Equatorial Africa (now Gabon).

about his childhood," [5] we get a curiously opposite picture of those early years, where the little boy ensconced in his grandfather's library "*plays the part*" of the young genius that his mother and grandparents wanted him to be. He describes his behaviour as play-acting – pretending to be a nascent writer and intellectual in order to please his elders, especially his grandfather Schweitzer, whom he termed "*God the Father,*" because of his imperious manner and imposing beard. "*Everything took place in my head,*" he confesses, "*imaginary child that I was, I defended myself with my imagination*" ("*Les Mots*" , p.71). That imagination, in both its creative and its critical functions, was to be Sartre's constant companion throughout his life. His own biography, like that of the other literary figures he would analyse, culminates in his explicit choice of the imaginary that he had implicitly "chosen" long before. [6]

Sartre spent his first five years with his mother in his grandparents' home, in the Parisian suburb of Meudon, and from 1911 in their Paris apartment near the Luxembourg Gardens. Sartre grew up extremely close to his mother. But she remarried, much to his regret, when he was twelve. From the fall of 1917 to the spring of 1920, Sartre lived with his mother and her new husband, Joseph Mancy, in La Rochelle on the southwest coast of France,

Educated in Paris

Sartre was raised and educated in Paris, except for what he depicts as a rather painful interlude in La Rochelle on the southwest coast of France, where he lived with his mother and her new husband, Joseph Mancy, for about two and a half years --- from the fall of 1917 to the spring of 1920. As a teenager in the 1920s, Sartre

---

[5] Cohen-Solal, Annie: "*Jean-Paul Sartre. A Life*", trans. Anna Concogni (New York: New Press, 2005), p. 40.

[6] Flynn, Thomas R.: "*The childhood of a genius*", Cambridge University Press, 2014, pp.3-4.

became attracted to philosophy upon reading Henri Bergson's essay '*Time and Free Will: An Essay on the Immediate Data of Consciousness*'. He attended the Cours Hattemer, a private school in Paris.

While in Paris, he attended two prestigious lycées [7] and the exclusive *École Normale Supérieure*. In 1915, while he was an extern at the *Lycée Henri IV*, he met Paul Nizan, who became one of his closest friends after his return to the lycée from La Rochelle in 1920, now as a boarder. After finishing their studies at *Henri IV*, Sartre and Nizan began the two-year course of study at the *Lycée Louis-le-Grand* (fall 1922–spring 1924) to prepare for the entrance exam to the *École Normale Supérieure* (ENS), an institution of higher education that was the alma mater for several prominent French thinkers and intellectuals. Sartre counted his four years at the ENS as being among the happiest phases of his life. It was there that he befriended Raymond Aron and Maurice Merleau-Ponty, as well as his lifelong companion Simone de Beauvoir who was a student at the Sorbonne, and also continued his association with Nizan. In fact, so close was his friendship with Nizan that their fellow *Normaliens* (from *École Normale Supérieure*) referred to the pair as "*Nitre et Sarzan*" (Nitre and Sarzan).

At the ENS, Sartre studied and earned certificates in psychology, history of philosophy, logic, general philosophy, ethics, sociology, and physics, as well as his *diplôme d'études supérieures* [fr] (roughly equivalent to an MA thesis). His 1928 MA thesis under the title "*L'Image dans la vie psychologique: rôle et nature*" ["Image in Psychological Life: Role and Nature"] was supervised by Henri Delacroix.

---

[7] The lycée (pronounced [lise]) is the second and last stage of secondary education in the French educational system.

Paul Nizan

Upon his graduation in 1928, Sartre sat for the philosophical agrégation, a national exam that qualified candidates to teach in lycées throughout the country. To everyone's amazement, Sartre failed the exam that year, but he emerged first (just ahead of de Beauvoir) in the competition the following year. After taking his agrege [8], Sartre went to Germany in 1933 to study under Edmund Husserl and Martin Heidegger, two of the most influential European philosophers, interested in the nature of being and reality and the mysteries of perception.

Sartre: The Teacher

"You have to talk to make sure you're alive."

— Jean-Paul Sartre, No Exit and Three Other Plays

[8] An academic rank conferred by a French university on one who has passed a rigidly competitive examination and who is therefore entitled to appointment to the highest teaching post in a lycée or in one of the faculties of a university.

From 1931 until 1945, i.e. till the conclusion of World War II, Sartre taught at various *lycees* of Le Havre (at the *Lycée de Le Havre*, , 1931–1936), Laon (at the Lycée de Laon, 1936–37), and, finally, Paris (at the *Lycée Pasteur*, 1937–1939, and at the *Lycée Condorcet*, 1941–1944). During this period, he began to publish philosophical works such as "*The Transcendence of the Ego*", "*The Imagination*", and "*The Emotions*", but the first book that brought him fame was a novel, "*Nausea*" (1938), which serves in some ways as a manifesto of '*existentialism'* and remains one of his most famous books. Written in the form of a diary, *Nausea* recounts the breakdown of the reassuring daily life of a young historian, Antoine Roquentin, who is staying in a western port city and working on the biography of a Revolution-era marquis. Roquentin feels nauseated as he experiences the absurdity normally hidden by his routines, and the truth of that absurdity appears ever more sharply as his life slowly gives way around him. As the attacks of nausea become more frequent, Roquentin abandons his research and thereafter finds and loses his few friends. He finds himself in an indifferent world, without love or friendship, in which he must discover value and meaning within himself.

In 1939, while he was teaching at the *Lycée Pasteur* in Paris, Sartre was drafted into the French army, where he served as a meteorologist. He was captured by German troops in 1940 in Padoux, and spent nine months as a prisoner of war. During this period, he wrote his first play *"Bariona, fils du tonnerre"* ('Bariona, Son of Thunder'), a drama concerning Christmas. It was during this period of confinement that Sartre read Martin Heidegger's Sein und Zeit, later to become a major influence on his own essay on phenomenological ontology. In April 1941, he was released because of his poor eyesight and exotropia that affected his balance. According to some biographers, he escaped after a medical visit to the ophthalmologist.

Back in Paris, Sartre recovered his teaching position at *Lycée Pasteur* near Paris and settled at the Hotel Mistral. In October 1941, he joined a position at l*ycée* Condorcet in Paris, replacing a Jewish teacher who had been forbidden to teach by anti-Jewish law (*'Vichy law'*) [9]. For this, Sartre's critics often scoff at him saying Sartre always lectured against anti-Semitism; but in actual practice, he did not hesitate to accept a position arising out of an anti-Semitic measure.

It was the period of Nazi occupation of Paris. During this period, Sartre was teaching, writing and working with the resistance. One of his plays produced during the Nazi occupation was "*The Flies*," an adaptation of the Greek legend of Orestes with subtle anti-Nazi overtones added.

His anti-Nazism later developed into anti-Stalinism. He visited the Soviet Union twice, in 1954 and 1962, but he also strongly denounced the Soviet government several times, notably in 1956 after the invasion of Hungary, and in the 1960s for the jailing of writers Yuli Daniel and Andrei Sinyavsky. An even more serious break came in 1968, after the quelling of the student uprising in Paris and the brutal suppression of the Dubcek regime in Czechoslovakia.

----

[9] 'Vichy rule' in France means the government of France after Germany defeated and occupied it at the beginning of World War II; Vichy, the capital, is a small city in central France. The Vichy government was essentially a puppet of the Germans.

Anti-Jewish laws were enacted by the Vichy France government in 1940 and 1941 affecting metropolitan France and its overseas territories during World War II. The statutes were aimed at depriving Jews of the right to hold public office, designating them as a lower class, and depriving them of citizenship. Many Jews were subsequently rounded up at Drancy internment camp before being deported for extermination in Nazi concentration camps.

The first Jewish status law dated 3 October 1940 excluded Jews from the army, press, commercial and industrial activities, and the civil service. The second status law was passed in July 1941 and required the registration of Jewish businesses and excluded Jews from any profession, commercial or industrial.

Chapter 2

Sartre: The Philosopher

"I would like **[people]** ***to remember Nausea, [my plays] No Exit and The Devil and the Good Lord, and then my two philosophical works, more particularly the second one, Critique of Dialectical Reason.. Then my essay on Genet, Saint Genet.... If these are remembered, that would be quite an achievement, and I don't ask for more."***

--- Jean-Paul Sartre

Sartreism

"We only become what we are by the radical and deep-seated refusal of that which others have made of us."

- **Jean-Paul Sartre**

Sartre has been dubbed the philosopher of the twentieth century.[1] He was a prolific writer. The '*Economist*' once calculated his output as twenty published pages per day of his working life ---- and diverse, including plays, short stories, novels, philosophical treatise, essays and reviews. His first novel, '*Nausea*' (1938), sold more than 1.6 million copies in his lifetime, and his play '*Dirty Hands*' (1948) nearly 2 million. Even his 700-page tome on phenomenological ontology, '*Being and Nothingness*', first published in 1943, went through five editions in its first three years and has never been out of print since. In addition to his memoir, '*Les Mots*' ['The Words'], 'he also left several autobiographical notebooks and diaries, as well as letters to and from his lifelong companion Simone de Beauvoir and other friends and lovers. [10]

The essence of Sartre's philosophy is that people, as humans, are "*condemned to be free*". "*This may seem paradoxical because condemnation is normally an external judgment which constitutes the conclusion of a judgment. Here, it is not the human who has chosen to be like this. There is a contingency of human existence. It is a condemnation of their being. Their being is not determined, so it is up to everyone to create their own existence, for which they are then responsible. They cannot not be free, there is a form of necessity for freedom, which can never be given up*." [11]

Sartre's theory is founded on the concept that there is no creator, and is illustrated using the example of a paper cutter. Sartre says that if one considered a paper cutter, one would assume that the creator would have had a plan for it: an essence. But the human beings, he argues, have no essence before their existence because there is no Creator (God). This forms the basis for his assertion human beings themselves are fully responsible for their actions. "*We are left alone, without excuse*." "*We can act without being determined by our past which is always separated from us*." [12]

Sartre maintained that the concepts of authenticity and individuality have to be earned and not learned. We need to experience "*death consciousness*" so as to wake up ourselves as to what is really important; the authentic in our lives which is life experience, not knowledge. [13] Death draws the final point when we

---

10 Bernard-Henri, Lévy, "*Sartre: The Philosopher of the Twentieth Century*", trans. Andrew Brown (London: Polity,2003.

11 Malinge, Yoann (2021). "*Sartre, "Existentialism is a humanism"*". The Literary Encyclopedia. Retrieved 12 May 2021 – via Academia.

12 Malinge, Yoann (2013). "*Does our past have a motivational effect? Our reasons for acting: Sartre's philosophy of action*". Vol. 4, no. 2. Ethics in Progress. pp. 46–53.

13 Sartre, Jean-Paul: "*Being and Nothingness*", Originally published 1943, Simon & Schuster; Reprint edition (1 August 1993), p. 246.

as beings cease to live for ourselves and permanently become objects that exist only for the outside world.

Sartre's philosophy was influenced by the German philosopher Martin Heidegger, but the publication of *Being and Nothingness* did mark a split in their perspectives, with Heidegger remarking in "*Letter on Humanism*" [14],

Martin Heidegger

> "*Existentialism says existence precedes essence. In this statement he is taking 'existentia' and 'essentia' according to their metaphysical meaning, which, from Plato's time on, has said that 'essentia' precedes 'existentia'. Sartre reverses this statement. But the reversal of a metaphysical statement remains a metaphysical statement. With it, he stays with metaphysics, in oblivion of the truth of Being.*" [15]

---

14 "*Letter on Humanism*" (German: *Über den Humanismus*) refers to a famous letter written by Martin Heidegger in December 1946 in response to a series of questions by Jean Beaufret (10 November 1946) about the development of French existentialism. Heidegger reworked the letter for publication in 1947. He distanced himself from Sartre's position and existentialism in general in this letter.

15 Heidegger, Martin "*Basic Writings from 'Being and Time' (1927) to 'The Task of Thinking' (1964)*", Routledge & Kegan Paul, 1978..

Herbert Marcuse also had issues with Sartre's opposition to metaphysics in *Being and Nothingness* and suggested the work projected anxiety and meaninglessness onto the nature of existence itself:

> "*Insofar as Existentialism is a philosophical doctrine, it remains an idealistic doctrine: it hypostatizes specific historical conditions of human existence into ontological and metaphysical characteristics. Existentialism thus becomes part of the very ideology which it attacks, and its radicalism is illusory.*" [16]

Sartre also took inspiration from phenomenological epistemology, explained by Franz Adler in this way:

> "*Man chooses and makes himself by acting. Any action implies the judgment that he is right under the circumstances not only for the actor, but also for everybody else in similar circumstances.*" [17]

Also important is Sartre's analysis of psychological concepts, including his suggestion that consciousness exists as something other than itself, and that the conscious awareness of things is not limited to their knowledge: for Sartre intentionality applies to the emotions as well as to cognitions, to desires as well as to perceptions.[18] "*When an external object is perceived, consciousness is also conscious of itself, even if consciousness is not its own object: it is a non-positional consciousness of itself.*" [19]

---

16 Marcuse, Herbert. "*Sartre's Existentialism*". Printed in Studies in Critical Philosophy. Translated by Joris De Bres. London: NLB, 1972. p. 161.

17 Adler, Franz (1949). "*The Social Thought of Jean-Paul Sartre*". American Journal of Sociology, 55 (3): pp. 284–294.

18 Farina, Gabriella (2014). "*Some reflections on the phenomenological method*", Archived 14 February 2019 at the Wayback Machine Dialogues in Philosophy, Mental and Neuro Sciences, 7(2): pp. 50–62.

19 Malinge, Yoann (2016). "Sartre, "*The Transcendance of the Ego*"", The Literary Encyclopedia. Retrieved 25 May 2019 – via Academia.

Sigmund Freud

However Sartre's critique of psychoanalysis, particularly of Freud, has faced some counter-critique. British philosophers Richard Wollheim and Thomas Baldwin argued that Sartre's attempt to show that Freud's theory of the unconscious is mistaken was based on a misinterpretation of Freud. [20] [21]

"Life begins on the other side of despair": Sartre

Jean-Paul Sartre had once said, "*Life begins on the other side of despair*"; it flows from Sartre's philosophy of Existentialism – and what it says is that to understand the life and to live it properly one has to go through a transformation – he has to experience various difficulties, impediments and even despair.

That our life has been decided for us by our socio-economic circumstances does not really mean that we are living our lives

[20] Wollheim, Richard. "*Freud*", London, Fontana Press, pp. 157–176.

[21] Baldwin, Thomas (1995). Ted Honderich (ed.). "*The Oxford Companion to Philosophy*", Oxford University Press. p. 792

without any responsibility of our own. In that case we would be just puppets, dancing with the strings that are being moved by the society. In order to live a life of our own, which is a true and productive, it is essential that we should create such a life. Creating a life means finding the true purpose of the existence and then acting in a manner so as to accomplish it. Creating such a life is not easy; it calls for, as pointed out earlier, a complete transformation. The transformation begins with negating what is already taught to human beings by his surroundings. One requires to un-condition and discover oneself and has to decide one's life according to one's own comprehension of one's self.

During this transformation, one may feel despair; and may experience nothingness. The world may look meaningless and purposeless. The roads may look dusty and leading to nowhere. The trees may look autumn-stricken and the water may be flowing in a purposeless manner. The relations may seem absurd and the friends may appear to be strangers. In the words of the American pastor and the author of The Purpose-Driven Life (2002) Rick Warren, "*Transformation is a process, and as life happens there are tons of ups and downs. It's a journey of discovery – there are moments on mountaintops and moments in deep valleys of despair.*" The important thing, however, is not to get stuck in this despair as the life is on the other side of despair. And this despair may also at times prove to be a necessary evil for it may induce a person to rethink about his life, to rewrite its script and to rebuild his personality. As the great novelist Dostoevsky once said, "*Suffering is the origin of consciousness.*"

Every individual is unique, Sartre says, in what he really is. Finding that unique self will require going through the quagmire of despair, and great revelations are waiting on the other side. Though going through this quagmire is necessary, sticking to it is to be avoided or, else it would lead to a useless and wasted life. The quagmire should be considered as just a necessary passage to the real destination on the other side of it.

Today's world wherein most of the people are lost in the pursuit of materialistic gains, it is a crying need that the human beings must discover themselves for proper understanding of the responsibilities and existence. He should suffer and despair, and then he has to take a rebirth. He has to be re-born as a different human being after going through the ocean of despair – *for life awaits him on the other side of despair.* [22]

1941 and thereafter: On Return from War service

On September 20, 1939, Sartre was conscripted into the French Army. Because of his exotropia [23], which he said caused him balance issues, and his partial blindness, he didn't go to the front. Instead, he was given the job of a meteorologist. It was, as he wrote in a letter to his friend and lifelong companion Simone de Beauvoir, "*extremely peaceful work; indeed I cannot think of any branch of the services that has a quieter, more poetic job—apart, that is, from the pigeon breeders, always supposing that nowadays there are any of them left.*"

"*My work here consists of sending up balloons and then watching them through a pair of field glasses,*" he explained. "*This is called `making a meteorological observation.' Afterwards I phone the battery artillery officers and tell them of the wind direction. What they do with this information is entirely their affair. The young ones make some intelligence reports based on it; the old school simply shove it in the wastepaper basket. In any event, since*

---

[22] Sherzai, Dilawar: "*Life begins on the other side of despair*", Daily Outlook, Afghanistan, September 04, 2014.

[23] Exotropia is a type of eye misalignment, where one eye deviates outward. The deviation may be constant or intermittent, and the deviating eye may always be one eye or may alternate between the two eyes.

there is no shooting here at present, either course is equally effective. As for me, I am left with a huge amount of spare time on my hands, which I am using to complete my novel." [24]

Jean-Paul Sartre

In 1940, Sartre was captured by German troops, and he had to spend nine months as a prisoner of war, during which time he also wrote a great deal, and passed the rest of the hours by reading Heidegger's "*Being and Time*". It was his eyes again that led to his release—or his escape, depending on who tells it. "*It wasn't a very swashbuckling escape, but it was simple and it worked,*" writes Sarah Bakewell in "*At the Existentialist Café*". [25]

He had been suffering a great deal from his eye problems, thanks to all the reading and writing—which were mostly done one-eyed. Sometimes both eyes were so sore that he tried to write with them closed, his handwriting wandering over the page. But his eyes gave him his escape route. Pleading the need for treatment, he procured a medical pass to visit an ophthalmologist outside the

[24] Temple, Emily: "*How Jean-Paul Sartre managed to spend his military service working on his novel* ", The Literary Hub, September 20, 2022

[25] Bakewell, Sarah: "*At the Existentialist Café: Freedom, Being, and Apricot Cocktails*", Chatto & Windus, March 3, 2016.

camp gates. Amazingly, believe it or not, he was then allowed to walk out, showing the pass, and he never went back.

The Second World War and his life in the army was a great educator for Sartre. "*That was when*", he later wrote, "*I made the transition from individualism and the pure individual ... to the social, to socialism*". The real world, he realized, was so different from the abstract world he lived in earlier, as an '*arm-chair philosopher*' or as a '*café de Flore intellectual*' – and that it was time for him to change.

Thus, on return to Paris, in May 1941, Sartre, with the help of de Beauvoir, tried to organise an underground group "*Socialisme et liberté*" ('*Socialism and Freedom*') along with other writers, like, Maurice Merleau-Ponty, Jean-Toussaint Desanti, Dominique Desanti, Jean Kanapa, and École Normale students. In spring of 1941, Sartre suggested with "cheerful ferocity" at a meeting that the "*Socialism and Freedom*" group members assassinate prominent war collaborators like Marcel Déat, but de Beauvoir noted that his idea was rejected as "*none of us* [members of the group] *felt qualified to make bombs or hurl grenades*". The British historian Ian Ousby observed that the French always had far more hatred for collaborators than they did for the Germans, noting it was French people like Déat [26] that Sartre wanted to assassinate rather than the military governor of France, General Otto von Stülpnagel, and the popular slogan always was "*Death to Laval*!" [27] rather than "*Death to Hitler*!".

---

[26] Marcel Déat (7 March 1894 – 5 January 1955) was a French politician. Initially a socialist and a member of the French Section of the Workers' International (SFIO); he led a breakaway group of right-wing 'Neosocialists' out of the SFIO in 1933. During the occupation of France by Nazi Germany, he founded the collaborationist National Popular Rally (RNP). [Source: Wikipedia]

[27] Pierre Jean Marie Laval (French pronunciation: [28 June 1883 – 15 October 1945) was a French politician. During the Third Republic, he served as Prime Minister of France from 27 January 1931 to 20 February 1932 and 7 June 1935 to 24 January 1936. He again occupied the post during the German occupation, from 18 April 1942 to 20 August 1944.

In August Sartre and de Beauvoir went to the French Riviera to seek the support of André Gide and André Malraux, but did not get adequate response. Being disappointed, Sartre decided to switch to writing instead of being involved in active resistance. He then wrote a number of classics including his principal philosophical work *"Being and Nothingness"* (1943), *"The Files"* (1943) and *"No exit"* (1944), none of which were censored by the Germans. This is why his critics sometimes allege that Sartre fraternised with the German censors to avoid censorship of his works.

Sartre also contributed to various literary magazines, including "*Combat*", a newspaper founded by his friend Albert Camus. After August, 1944 and the "*Liberation of Paris*", he wrote "*Anti-Semite and Jew*" (1944) in which he tried to explain the causes of "*hate*" in reference to the Jews.

In 1945, after the war ended, Sartre quit teaching and devoted his time to writing and political activism. It is then he wrote his famous trilogy of novels, "*Les Chemins de la Liberté*" ('*The Roads to Freedom*') – comprising *"Age of Reason"* (1945), *"The Reprieve"* (1945) and *"Troubled Sleep"* (1949).

Years later, in 1975, shortly before his death, when Sartre was asked how he would like to be remembered, he replied:

> *"I would like [people] to remember Nausea, [my plays] No Exit and The Devil and the Good Lord, and then my two philosophical works, more particularly the second one, Critique of Dialectical Reason.. Then my essay on Genet, Saint Genet.... If these are remembered, that would be quite an achievement, and I don't ask for more."*

……….

Chapter 3

Sartre: The Political Activist

"The task of the intellectual is not to decide where there are battles but to join them wherever and whenever the people wage them. Commitment is an act, not a word."

- Jean-Paul Sartre

Sartre's classic period as a philosopher continued till the early 1940s. The war politicized him.

In 1945, after the war ended, Sartre moved to an apartment on the rue Bonaparte, where he was to produce most of his subsequent work and where he lived until 1962. It was from there that he helped establish a quarterly literary and political review, '*Les Temps modernes*' (Modern Times), in part to popularize his thought. He ceased teaching and devoted his time to writing and political activism.

1945: Sartre visits USA

In early 1945, with the war not yet over, Sartre visited the United States for the first time. He travelled with a group of correspondents who were invited for the sake of influencing French public opinion favourably toward the United States. Sartre was sent by his friend Albert Camus to report back to '*Combat*', the leading newspaper of the independent left that had emerged from the Resistance. Once invited, Sartre arranged also to report back to the conservative newspaper *Le Figaro*. de Beauvoir said that learning of Camus's invitation in late 1944 was one of the most exciting moments of Sartre's life.

Known before the war for *Nausea* (1938) and *The Wall* (1939), Sartre's reputation as an intellectual had grown further by the time he was scheduled to visit the US with the performance of his plays *The Flies* (1943) and *No Exit* (1944) during the Occupation, and with the publication of his seminal work *Being and Nothingness* during the same period. He had also made several contributions to *Les Lettres Françaises*, [28] published clandestinely.

Twenty articles authored by Sartre about his American trip were published in *Combat* (February 2 to June 30) and a dozen in *Le Figaro* (January 24 to July 30). Seven of the articles from *Le Figaro* based on his 1945 US trip (gathered as "*Individualism and Conformism in the United States*" and "*American Cities*") were published in '*Situations*' and later translated into English in '*Literary and Philosophical Essays*'. But none of the *Combat* articles has ever been republished in French or translated into any other language. The articles on the U. S. working class appeared after Sartre returned home in May, appearing from June 6 to June 30, 1945. [29]

Sartre's visit came just about the beginning of the post-war "honeymoon" period between the USA and the USSR. They had effectively divided the world between them and for the moment neither side wanted to upset the balance. Things, however, changed dramatically in 1947, with the "Truman Doctrine," the exclusion of

---

[28] "*Les Lettres Françaises*" was a French literary publication, founded in 1941 by writers Jacques Decour and Jean Paulhan. Originally a clandestine magazine of the French Resistance in German-occupied territory, it was one of the many publications of the National Front resistance movement. [Source: Wikipedia]

[29] "Sartre, Jean-Paul: "*Sartre on the American Working Class: Seven Articles in Combat from 6 to 30 June, 1945.*", Sartre Studies International, Vol. 6, Issue 1, 2000

Communist ministers from the French government and American support—political and financial—for France's war in Indochina.

Sartre (third from left) and other French journalists visit General George C. Marshall in the Pentagon, 1945

Sartre had quite a positive view of US society. He made a number of contacts on the American left, especially those around the journals '*Partisan Review and Politics*'. American writers—like the black ex-Communist Richard Wright—contributed to '*Les Temps Modernes*'. Sartre did not fail to notice some of the fundamental divisions in US society—above all those of class and race. But it was class organization above all that offered hope for the future; he argued that "*when the American proletariat—black and white—has recognized the identity of its interests in face of the employing class, the Negroes will struggle with white workers and on an equal footing with them for the recognition of their rights. It is from the workers' organizations, and from them alone, that blacks can hope for effective assistance.*"

Sartre was widely criticized for being anti-American because he had drawn attention to racism in American society. In the light of later developments, especially the civil rights movement, it is now apparent Sartre was right to give due importance to the place of racist oppression in American society.

Cold War politics: Sartre leans towards Marxism

In the early 1950s, when the Cold War was at its peak as the world was increasingly perceived as split into communist and capitalist blocs, Sartre developed interest in Marxism though he did not join the Communist party. Sartre wrote in support of the secret Resistance groups that had sprung up throughout the German occupied Europe during the Nazi rule and was highly critical of collaborators and those who had remained passive during the German occupation. He sought to glorify the Resistance after the war as the uncompromising expression of morality in action, and was of the view that the "*résistants*" were a "*band of brothers*" who had enjoyed "*real freedom*" in a way that did not exist before nor after the war. He did not spare attacking anyone who had collaborated or remained passive during the German occupation; he even criticized Camus, then his bosom friend, for signing an appeal to spare the collaborationist writer Robert Brasillach from being executed. In the late 1940s, Sartre described French nationalism as "*provincial*" and in a 1949 essay, he advocated for a *"United States of Europe*". [30]

He did not remain confined as a mere arm-chair theoretical sympathiser but permitted himself to be arrested for ultra-leftist causes; these arrests, however, did not result in jail terms. His voice

---

[30] Bondy, Francois:. "*Jean-Paul Sartre and Politics*". The Journal of Contemporary History. Vol. 2 No.2, April 1967, pp. 25–48.

became more strident, and he lectured his fellow thinkers to join class warfare wherever and whenever the people wage them: [31]

> "*The task of the intellectual is not to decide where there are battles but to join them wherever and whenever the people wage them. Commitment is an act, not a word.*"

About the Korean War (25 Jun 1950 – 27 Jul 1953), Sartre accused the South Korean feudalists and the Americans for promoting the war. But he also believed it was begun by the North Koreans.

But the same year in 1950, when the Korean War began, David Rousset, a former political ally of Sartre and himself the survivor of a Nazi camp, launched a campaign against concentration camps in the USSR. Sartre, however, somewhat in violation of his own stated principle, refused to support his cause, on the ground that the campaign was being waged in the right-wing press, and that it failed to oppose camps in right-wing, pro-American regimes.

For a pretty long period, Sartre strongly believed Soviet Union was a "*revolutionary*" state struggling for the betterment of humanity. After an official visit to Soviet Union in 1954, just after Stalin's death, he declared he found "*complete freedom of criticism*" there and that the Soviet citizen was "*constantly improving his way of life in the midst of a society that is making constant progress*". On the contrary, he condemned the United States for sinking into "*prefascism*". About the Soviet writers expelled from the Soviet Writers' Union, Sartre was blunt to observe that they *"still had the opportunity of rehabilitating themselves by writing better books"*

---

[31] Whitman, 97:" Jean-Paul Sartre, 74, Dies in Paris", New York Times, April 16, 1980.

Sartre & de Beauvoir at Vilnius airport, Lithuania, 1965

Chapter 4
Anti-colonial movement and Jean-Paul Sartre

"There is one duty to be done, one end to achieve: to thrust out colonialism by every means in their power."

-- Jean-Paul Sartre, Preface to Frantz Fanon's "Wretched of the Earth"

Anti-colonial movement: Sartre advocates for outright independence of European-held African and Asian colonies

In the two hundred years following the American Revolutionary War in 1783, 165 colonies have gained independence from Western imperial powers. [32] Several analyses point to different reasons for the spread of anti-colonial political movements. Institutional arguments suggest that increasing levels of education in the colonies led to calls for popular sovereignty; Marxist analyses view decolonisation as a result of economic shifts toward wage labor and an enlarged bourgeois class; yet another argument sees decolonisation as a diffusion process wherein earlier revolutionary movements inspired later ones. Other explanations emphasize how the lower profitability of colonization and the costs associated with empire prompted decolonization. [33]

---

[32] Strang, David: "*Global patterns of decolonisation, 1500–1987*", International Studies Quarterly (1991), pp. 429–454.

[33] Gartzke, Erik; Rohner, Dominic (2011). "*The Political Economy of Imperialism, Decolonization and Development*". British Journal of Political Science. 41 (3), pp.525–556.

The process of decolonisation gathered momentum after World War I and got further accelerated following the Second World war with the emergence of the USA and the Soviet Union as two new superpowers. [34] Ironically, few European intellectuals concerned themselves with this dissolution of the imperial projects across the Global South in the mid-20th century; even fewer advocated outright for the independence of European-held African and Asian colonies. Sartre was perhaps the most influential member of this latter group and began writing on anticolonial resistance since the late 1940s. As an anti-colonialist, he-was all out against the use of torture and concentration camps by the French in Algeria.

After the outbreak of the Algerian War of Independence in 1954, Sartre became a vocal proponent of the *Front de Libération Nationale* (FLN), the Algerian nationalist group that waged armed struggle for liberation. Sartre famously condemned the French military's widespread, systemic use of torture on FLN members and Algerian civilians, and backed unconditional independence for the colony. Because of his views, he became a target of the right-wing paramilitary Organisation '*Armée Secrète*' (OAS, Secret Armed Organisation) escaping two bomb attacks in the early '60s. He later argued in 1959 that each French person was responsible for the collective crimes during the Algerian War of Independence.

After Algeria's victory in 1962, Sartre remained steadfast in his anticolonial activism; he would write on topics such as the Cuban Revolution, US intervention in Vietnam and unjust French immigration policies.

---

[34] In 1945, France's colonial empire, the second largest in the world, covered nearly one tenth of the world's land area, and five percent of the world's population. By 1962, it was almost gone.

Atrocities in French Colonies: Sartre takes a stand against the Empire

Jean-Paul Sartre came to prominence just as France was trying to cling onto its empire in a series of bloody wars. He used his platform as a public intellectual to speak out bravely against colonial repression, risking his own life in the process.

In the immediate aftermath of World War II, a weakened France, whose status as a sovereign nation was in question, unleashed a series of desperate, bloody, and temporarily successful attempts to reassert control over its colonies. Ironically, all these happened at a time when France itself had recently been under Nazi occupation by Germany.

In January 1944, Charles de Gaulle rallied Africans to his side by virtually promising independence during a famous speech in Brazzaville, the capital of French-ruled Congo. Emboldened by this assurance of liberation, and by France's military defeats in Europe, the people in many French colonies took to the streets demanding sovereignty and their own liberation.

On the 8th May 1945, *the Victory in Europe Day* [35], in the Algerian towns of Sétif and Guelma, hundreds of people demonstrated under the Algerian flag. Riots ensued, the French authorities lost control, and some police officers and settlers were killed. The repression that followed was ruthless; a series of massacres by the French police killed thousands of Arab civilians; even by conservative estimates, there were at least ten thousand Algerian victims. This bloodbath was a permanent trauma for the

---

[35] 'Victory in Europe' Day is the day celebrating the formal acceptance by the Allies of World War II of Germany's unconditional surrender of its armed forces on Tuesday, 8 May 1945, marking the official end of World War II in Europe in the Eastern Front, with the last shots fired on the 11th. [Source: Wikipedia]

Algerians: in effect, the country's war of independence came out of it. [36]

About two years later, in March 1947, the French army perpetrated another massacre in Madagascar, killing tens of thousands of Malagasies when they tried to assert their independence. It was at a time when France was still reeling from the Nazi occupation. Similar attempts of uprise against colonial order in Senegal, Cameroon, and Syria, each of which were ruthlessly repressed by the French armed forces or by settlers. In French-ruled Indochina, a French naval ship bombarded the city of Haiphong in November 1946, killing six thousand people, inaugurating a full-scale war against the independence movement led by Ho Chi Minh.

At this point of time, virtually no public intellectual denounced the actions of the French Government. [37] Jean-Paul Sartre was an exception. Sartre's first public reaction to France's colonial war in Indochina came in December 1946, in a *Les Temps Modernes* editorial titled "*Both Executioners and Victims*." It was a rebuttal of Albert Camus's article series "*Neither Victims nor Executioners*," which had condemned revolutionary violence from a pacifist standpoint. The editorial broke with all the French parliamentary parties, including the Communist Party, which was part of the ruling coalition at the time. It denounced the Indochina war and called for the withdrawal of French troops.

Sartre's editorial went to the extent of justifying revolutionary violence and compared the French presence in Indochina to the German occupation of France, which provoked the outrage of many commentators. French novelist and critic François Mauriac wrote a scathing article in response, attacking Sartre directly. Taking the

---

[36] Gloag, Oliver: "*Jean-Paul Sartre Took a Stand Against Empire*". Jacobin.

[37] Other than the Surrealists, who condemned the Indochina war.

side of Sartre, the Martinican poet Aimé Césaire later elaborated upon Sartre's comparison of French colonial crimes with those of Nazi Germany in his work "*Discours sur le Colonialisme*". Césaire criticized the deliberate distinction being made in Europe using terms such as 'massacres' and 'conquests', depending on the location and nationality of the victims. Sartre's own critique of French colonialism would also soon go beyond his radical humanist perspective and come to resemble Césaire's.

Aimé Césaire

Chapter 5
Negritude, Black Orpheus and Jean-Paul Sartre

"The claim to a national culture in the past does not only rehabilitate that nation and serve as a justification for the hope of a future national culture. In the sphere of psycho-affective equilibrium it is responsible for an important change in the native."

- Frantz Fanon, "The Wretched of the Earth"

Negritude

The dream and desire for political freedom amongst the colonial subjects was preceded by an urge on their part to establish a literary and cultural identity of their own. In May 1935, the word '*Négritude'* appeared for the first time in the only issue of the literary magazine '*L'Etudiant noir'*, edited by Léopold Sédar Senghor, Aimé Césaire and Léon-Gontran Damas. Négritude was defined it as "*the simple recognition of the fact that one is black*" and transcended the borders of the black Francophone literary world. [38]

The idea gathered momentum and soon it gave birth to the international literary movement, '*Negritude',* for which Paris, in 1937, with its diverse and tolerant art scene, became the centre of

[38] Nigerian Nobel Prize winner Wole Soyinka, the first African laureate to win the prize in 1986, countered the idea with his famous quote, "*A tiger does not shout its tigritude, it pounces.*"

the movement. In the face of growing fascism, black students, scholars and artists from French colonies in Africa and the Caribbean got together with the aim of promoting an appreciation of the history and culture of black people. They also wanted to draw attention to the experience of those who had lived under colonial rule, including slavery.

Négritude was led by the Martinican poet Aimé Césaire, French Guianese poet Léon Damas and the future Senegalese President and poet laureate Léopold Sédar Senghor. It was influenced by a range of styles and art movements including surrealism and the Harlem Renaissance. With the outbreak of the Second World War and the dispersal of its artists and intellectuals from Paris, Négritude became a global art movement.

After the war Paris again became the centre for Négritude activities. Many artists from Africa and the Caribbean came to Europe to study and gravitated to Paris, meeting at the *Clamart* tea-shop, the Négritude base on the Left Bank. Among these were London students Frank Bowling, Aubrey Williams, Donald Locke, Ben Enwonwu and Uzo Egonu.

In the immediate postwar period, Sartre listened to voices from outside the city of Paris and treated them with considerable importance. His first text dealing directly with the French empire as a system was a short presentation titled "*Présence Noire*" ('Black Presence') for the magazine *Présence Africaine* ('African presence') in the fall of 1947. [39] In this text, Sartre attacked the hypocrisy of the metropolitan French who considered themselves to be tolerant and understanding because they socialized with black men in the metropole. But what about those in the colonies, he asked? And what about the exploitation and misery to be found

[39] '*Présence Africaine*' was a publication founded by the Senegalese writer Alioune Diop that quickly became the main voice for the négritude movement.

there? Who remain responsible for the miseries heaped on these poor souls?

Negritude, Black Orpheus and Jean-Paul Sartre

"When you removed the gag that was keeping these black mouths shut, what were you hoping for? That they would sing your praises? Did you think that when they raised themselves up again, you would read adoration in the eyes of these heads that our fathers had forced to bend down to the very ground? Here are black men standing, looking at us, and I hope that you – like me --- will feel the shock of being seen. For three thousand years, the white man has enjoyed the privilege of seeing without being seen; he was only a look --- the light from his eyes drew each thing out of the shadow of birth; the whiteness of his skin was another look, condensed light. The white man – white because he was man, white like daylight – white like truth, white like virtue --- lighted up the creation like a torch and unveiled the secret white essence of beings. Today the black men are looking at us, and our gaze comes back to our own eyes; in their turn, the black torches light up the world and our white heads are no more than Chinese lanterns swinging in the wind. A black poet -- unconcerned with us – whispers to the woman he loves:

> ***"Naked woman. black woman***
> ***Dressed in your color which is life …***
> ***"Naked woman. dark woman,***
> ***Firm fleshed ripe fruit, somber ecstasies of black wine.***

and our whiteness seems to us to be a strange livid varnish that keeps our skin from breathing? white tights, worn out at the elbows and knees, under which we would find real human flesh the color of black wine if we could remove them. We think we are

essential to the world? suns of its harvests, moons of its tides; we are no more than its fauna, beasts. Not even beasts:

> ***These gentlemen from the city***
> ***These proper gentlemen***
> ***Who no longer know how to dance in the evening by moonlight***
> ***Who no longer know how to walk on the flesh of their feet***
> ***Who no longer know how to tell tales by the fireside . . .***

Formerly Europeans with divine right, we were already feeling our dignity beginning to crumble under American or Soviet looks; Europe was already no more than a geographical accident, the peninsula that Asia shoves into the Atlantic. We were hoping at least to find a bit of our greatness reflected in the domesticated eyes of the Africans. But there are no more domesticated eyes: there are wild and free looks that judge our world.

-- Jean-Paul Sartre, "Orphee noir" ('Black Orpheus) [40]

In 1948, Sartre wrote "*Orphee Noir*" ["Black Orpheus"], an essay on the "*Négritude*" movement and its role in the global struggle for decolonization and freedom. He identified Négritude as an empowering force for the colonized African, a necessary vehicle to "[draw] *himself erect and proudly* [proclaim] *himself a black man, face to face with white men,*" in preparation for a coming universal revolution. Several currents of Négritude existed, and in this essay, Sartre associated with Léopold Senghor, first president and Poet Laureate of Senegal. who praised African existence and

[40] "*Orphee Noir*" appeared originally as the preface to an anthology of African and West Indian poets, edited by Leopold Sedar-Senghor (*Anthologie de la nouvelle poesie negre et malgache de langue francais*, Paris, 1948). A key document in the history of the concept of "*Negritude*," it has been available in English only in a difficult to come by and out-of-print issue of *Presence Africaine* (Paris, 1951). It appeared in '*Massachusetts Review'* in its first American publication with the permission of M. Sartre, in a translation by John MacCombie.

epistemology as essentially more in line with the rhythms of nature; at one point he refers to the black peasant as "*the great male of the earth, the world's sperm*," whose purpose is "*to till, to plant, to eat... to make love with nature*." At another instance, he asserts full-on African essentialism when he describes the "*essence of blackness in the well of* [the black man's] *heart*."

Leopold Senghor

"*Black Orpheus*" is still considered an important intervention in Africana philosophy, and more widely, non-western thought. Nevertheless, it came in for criticism by Fanon, who challenged Sartre's analysis of Négritude in his first book, "*Black Skin, White Masks*".

Frantz Fanon

Sartre, however, wrote the preface for Fanon's magnum opus, "*Wretched of the Earth*", which was published shortly before Fanon succumbed to leukemia in December of 1961. The work drew devotees across Africa, Asia, and South America across the 1960s-1970s: its release, together with the FLN's victory in Algeria and Fanon's untimely death, exalted the West Indian psychiatrist to the pantheon of Third World luminaries. Stuart Hall observed that the book was the "*Bible for decolonization*," and the myth of Fanon and his revolutionary work still proliferates in the present day. Sartre's preface lent Fanon's oeuvre credibility and enabled its dissemination across the western world. [41]

In the light of the above, there's hardly any doubt that Sartre played an important role in the fight for decolonization, going far beyond his peers in advocating on behalf of the colonized,

[41] Alaigh, Arvin: " Black Skin, White ally: The complicated relationship of Jean -Paul Sartre and Frantz Fanon",
https://africasacountry.com/2018/08/black-skin-white-ally]

subjugated and wretched of the earth. Congolese philosopher, professor, and author V. Y. Mudimbe goes as far as to call Sartre an "*African Philosopher*" for all his contributions to the struggle.

Chapter 6
Jean-Paul Sartre and the Palestine Question

"If the Jew had not existed, the anti-Semite would have invented him"

--- Jean-Paul Sartre, "Anti-Semite and Jew"

Sartre died more than 40 years ago. Despite his fervent support for the Arab world, the Palestinian cause remains a blemish on his political and intellectual record.

Algeria had opted for independence in a referendum on July 1, 1962. On July 3, 1962, France recognized Algeria as an independent state. The same day, on July 3, 1962, United States recognized Algeria when President John Kennedy issued a congratulatory message to the Algerian people upon their independence from France. For his sustained intellectual support to their cause for independence, Jean-Paul Sartre, the 57-year old French intellectual rock star, living in a small apartment on the Left bank in Paris, was a darling of the Algerian people at that time.

But, five years after independence, in June Algerian students set fire to the books of Jean-Paul Sartre; Sartre, who had been a great friend of the Algerian revolution. A ban of Sartre's books was also announced in Iraq, and Arab intellectuals across the board began disavowing their kinship with the philosopher from the Paris Left Bank. It was a dramatic change from the earlier scenario when by the late 1950s the Arab world would boast of having the largest existentialist scene outside Europe. Indeed, almost everything that Sartre said and wrote during those years was translated to Arabic as soon as it hit the French market.

Around the same time, Josie Fanon, widow of the anti-colonialist essayist Frantz Fanon, asked his publisher to remove Sartre's forward to her husband's book '*The Wretched of the Earth'*.

> "*From now on, there is absolutely nothing in common between Sartre and us,*" she declared.

The reason for all these was Sartre's public support for Israel in the '*Six-Day War*'. Fanon's widow, Josie considered Sartre's pro-Israel stance as inconsistent with the anti-colonialist position of the book, so she omitted the preface. When interviewed at Howard University in 1978, she explained "*when Israel declared war on the Arab countries* [during the Six-Day War], *there was a great pro-Zionist movement in favour of Israel among western* (French) *intellectuals. Sartre took part in this movement. He signed petitions favouring Israel. I felt that his pro-Zionist attitudes were incompatible with Fanon's work*". [42]

By coming out in favour of Israel on the eve of the 1967 '*Six-Day War*', Sartre practically put an end to the Arab existentialist movement, discrediting in one stroke his revolutionary stance on the struggles for freedom across the Middle East and North Africa.

His stance marked a radical departure from his earlier one on the Jewish question. In an essay entitled "*Antisemite and Jew*", [43] he had written: "*It is the antisemite who creates the Jew ... who compels the Jew to make himself a Jew in spite of himself.*"

But in 1967, the same Sartre wrote in '*Les Temps Modernes*', a journal he co-founded with Simone de Beauvoir.

---

[42] Recent reprints of Fanon's book have, however, generally included Sartre's preface. [Source: Wikipedia]

[43] "*Anti-Semite and Jew*" is an essay about antisemitism written by Jean-Paul Sartre shortly after the Liberation of Paris from German occupation in 1944.

> *"Thus are we allergic to whatever may resemble, in one way or another, antisemitism. Many Arabs will reply: 'We are not antisemitic but anti-Israeli.' And they are no doubt correct: but they cannot keep us from thinking that those Israelis are also Jews,"*

Throughout the 1950s, Sartre was silent on the Israeli-Palestinian conflict. At the same time, he had lent his full support in favour of Algerian independence. During this period, he was the darling of the Arab intelligentsia, won over by his strong views and the image he had honed of being a committed intellectual. From Algiers and Baghdad to Cairo, Damascus and Beirut, he was one of the most widely translated, debated and celebrated intellectuals.

But after the independence of Algeria in 1962, Sartre could no longer avoid the Palestine question. Torn between his political convictions and his "emotional determination", Sartre chose an ambivalent stance. On the one hand, he consistently condemned the living conditions of Palestinian refugees and championed their right of return; on the other hand, he supported the existence of Israel as a sovereign state. These apparently contradictory efforts to remain "neutral" entailed a crisis of confidence. [44]

1967: Sartre visits Egypt

In February 1967, Sartre visited Egypt, Gaza and Israel to investigate the conflict, and spoke on the subject with the students, activists, refugees, women, workers and party members, including Egyptian President Gamal Abdel Nasser. It was a visit loaded with heavy political consequences, with both sides of the conflict vying for the celebrated French philosopher's support. Everything he said was picked apart, analysed and interpreted as a possible sign of

---

[44] Merida, Reda:" *On Jean-Paul Sartre and Palestine*", Middle East Eye, 20 May 2020.

support. Meanwhile, more and more editorials and statements urging Sartre to take a firm stand were being published by Arab intellectuals, who saw his apparent neutrality as a sign of support for Israel.

Egyptian President Gamal Abdel Nasser (left) greets Sartre (centre) in Cairo in 1967

Hike in tension between Egypt and Israel: Sartre signs petition in support of Israel

Shortly after Sartre's visit, tensions between Egypt and Israel led to a military escalation in the region that garnered considerable support in France in favour of Israel which, amid associations of former combatants and returnees from French Algeria, turned into a racist, anti-Arab campaign. In this context, a petition in support of Israel was published in *Le Monde*. Sartre was among the signatories, proclaiming in black and white the French philosopher's breakup with his Arab friends. Only later would they learn that Sartre had been loath to sign

Sartre (second from right) and Simone de Beauvoir (right) visit a Palestinian refugee camp in Gaza in 1967

From the 1970s onwards, however, with the intensification and export of the Palestinian struggle in Europe, the opinions of left-wing intellectuals on Israel underwent a spectacular reversal. Sartre would even go so far as to support suicide attacks.

> *"I have always supported counterterror against established terror. And I have always defined established terror as occupation, land seizure, arbitrary arrest, and so on,"* he noted.

Israel was no longer seen as an island surrounded by hostile Arab waters, but as a cog in the US imperial machine - and an over-militarised cog, to boot, attacking a people crushed by centuries of Ottoman, and later British, occupation.

Simone de Beauvoir and Sartre with local activists and intellectuals in the Egyptian village of Kamshish, February 1967.[45]

Sartre's Rejoinder: I'm Not against Palestinian Struggle for freedom

The interesting question here is how did this political reversal come about? Sartre, who had retreated into silence after the controversy, said in an interview given to the Egyptian newspaper *Al-Ahram*, and which appeared in the Lebanese existentialist magazine *Al-Adab*, in the months following the publication of the controversial petition, that his signature was only a stand "*against*

[45] Following the visit of Simone de Beauvoir and Sartre with local activists and intellectuals in February, 1967, the village of Kamshish became famous as a site of successful grass-root socialist struggle to reclaim land from the hands of feudalist. {See: de-Capua, Yoav: "*The Great Betrayal: Jean-Paul Sartre and the Arabs*", Not Even Past, April 1, 2018.

the looming [Six-Day] *war*" and not against the Arab and Palestinian people's "*struggle* for freedom and progress".

In a bid to sound authentic and sincere, he condemned Israel's use of napalm, which he described as a "*criminal act*"; he recalled why French public opinion had been favourable to Israel in the 1967 war, claiming that the French stance had been fuelled by fears of witnessing a second "*attempt to exterminate the Jews*" and by ignorance about what was really going on.

He also declared that "*wars of liberation are the only legitimate wars*", condemning Israel's expansionist intentions and describing the plan to annex Jerusalem as "*absolute madness*". Lastly, he said he regretted the "*powerful reactionary forces*" gaining ground in Israel and preventing all possibility of peace.

In 1976, he was awarded an honorary doctorate from the Hebrew University of Jerusalem. In his acceptance speech, he said he would have likewise been honoured to receive such a title from the University of Cairo. [46]

In 1979, he organised a seminar for the advancement of peace in the Middle East in which both Israeli and Palestinian intellectuals were invited. But his position on Israel, however, possibly continued to remain a matter not above suspicion.

----

[46] Ibid., 41.

Chapter 7
Sartre: A Staunch critic of Injustice

"It disturbs me no more to find men base, unjust, or selfish than to see apes mischievous, wolves savage, or the vulture ravenous."

--- Jean-Paul Sartre

The main enemy is at home

In 1952, in the new era of cold war politics, Sartre shifted his own position in the domestic politics within France. The French police had at that time viciously attacked a Communist demonstration, and the PCF's acting leader was arrested for being in possession of two pigeons, with which, it was alleged, he was planning to communicate with Moscow. There was even talk of banning the party altogether.

In this backdrop, when many of the PCF's former supporters were breaking their links with the party, Sartre announced his alliance with it on the ground that the PCF had massive working-class support (about five million voters), and Sartre wished to stand by the organized working class. For him, he said, what was happening in France was more important than what was happening in the USSR: in the words of the German Communist Karl Liebknecht, *"the main enemy is at home."*

1955: Sartre and de Beauvoir visit China

In 1955, de Beauvoir and Sartre visited China on a six-week trip on the occasion of the 6th Anniversary of Founding of

Communist China in Beijing. The visit was in response to Chou En-Lai's invitation at the Bandung Conference of non-aligned nations, where the first premier of the People's Republic had challenged the world to "*come and see*" what the Chinese revolution had achieved. De Beauvoir and Sartre, along with many others on the European left, took him up on it; they were among some 1,500 foreign delegates to the festivities celebrating the 6th anniversary of the revolution in October of that year. As French surrealist writer Leiris, who was also a part of the delegation, observed, this was a "*voyage engagé*"—a committed, engaged voyage: "*To participate in this organized delegation was implicitly to declare oneself a sympathizer.*"

Simone de Beauvoir and Jean-Paul at the 6th Anniversary of Founding of Communist China in Beijing 1955

A Staunch critic of abuses of freedom and human rights --- anywhere, everywhere

Though a Marxist, Sartre was generally critical of abuses of freedom and human rights anywhere and everywhere, including by the Soviet Union. He condemned the '*labour camps*' in USSR, and vehemently opposed Russian anti-Semitism, and the execution of dissidents.

In 1956, Sartre turned his back on Soviet Communism, as he disapproved of the brutal Russian intervention in Hungary. *"Soviets in Hungary were acting like Americans",* he said. When the Soviet leadership sent tanks into Hungary to crush a working-class rising, Sartre's opposition was forthright and public, insisting that socialism "*is not brought at bayonet point*." Thereafter, his criticism of the USSR became ever sharper: he condemned "*Soviet imperialism*," and argued that the Soviet working classes should "*take the power which has been stolen from them*" by the country's rulers. [47]

Sartre also admired the Polish leader Wladyslaw Gomulka who advocated a "*Polish road to socialism*" and wanted more independence for

---

[47] Strangely, however, the same year, in 1956, Sartre also attacked Nikita Khrushchev's "*Secret Speech*" delivered after the death of Stalin, which condemned the Stalinist repressions and purges. Sartre argued that "*the masses were not ready to receive the truth*". In 1973 he argued that "*revolutionary authority always needs to get rid of some people that threaten it, and their death is the only way*". A number of people, starting from Frank Gibney in 1961, classified Sartre as a "*useful idiot*" due to his uncritical position.

Wladyslaw Gomułka's speech, Warsaw, 1956

Poland, but was loyal to the Soviet Union. Sartre's newspaper '*Les Temps Modernes*' devoted a number of special issues in 1957 and 1958 to Poland under Gomulka, praising him for his reforms.

Critics have pointed out the contradiction between Sartre's "*ultra-Bolshevism*" stand as he expressed admiration for the Chinese leader Mao Zedong as the man who lead the oppressed masses of the Third World into revolution and at the same time praising a moderate Communist leader like Gomulka.

During the time of the "*May Revolution*" in Paris in the summer of 1968, a volatile period of civil disobedience marked by demonstrations and massive general strikes as well as the occupation of universities and factories, Sartre stood up for the issues of radical left-wing student groups for which he was arrested. President Charles de Gaulle intervened and pardoned him, commenting that "*you don't arrest Voltaire*". [48]

---

48 Bishop, Tom: "*Superstar of the Mind*", The New York Times, 7 June 1987.

Jean-Luc Godard, Jean-Paul Sartre, and Simone de Beauvoir gather to distribute copies of the Maoist newspaper '*La Cause du Peuple*' on the street after it is banned by the government (Paris, 1970)

He also strongly opposed the U.S. involvement in Vietnam war and, along with Bertrand Russell and others, organized a tribunal to expose U.S. war crimes, which became known as the "*Russel Tribunal*" in 1967. [49]

---

[49] The Russell Tribunal, also known as the International War Crimes Tribunal, Russell–Sartre Tribunal, or Stockholm Tribunal, was a private People's Tribunal organised in 1966 by the British philosopher and Nobel Prize winner Bertrand Russell, and hosted by French philosopher and writer Jean-Paul Sartre, along with Lelio Basso, Simone de Beauvoir, Vladimir Dedijer, Ralph Schoenman, Isaac Deutscher and several others. The tribunal investigated and evaluated American foreign policy and military intervention in Vietnam.

Russell Tribunal: Nine-year-old Do Van Ngoc exhibits injuries from napalm bombs dropped in Vietnam

'Critique de la raison dialectique' ('Critique of Dialectical Reason')

Sartre's work after Stalin's death, the '*Critique de la raison dialectique*' ('Critique of Dialectical Reason'), appeared in 1960, a second volume appearing posthumously. In the Critique, Sartre gave Marxism a more vigorous intellectual defence than it had received until then. He ended by concluding that Marx's notion of "*class*" as an objective entity was fallacious. Sartre's emphasis on the humanist values in the early works of Marx led to a dispute with Louis Althusser, a leading leftist intellectual in France in the 1960s, who claimed that the ideas of the young Marx were decisively superseded by the "*scientific*" system of the later Marx.

In the late 1950s, Sartre began to argue that the European working classes were too apolitical to carry out the revolution predicated by Marx, that it was the impoverished masses of the Third World, the "*real damned of the earth*", who would carry out the revolution. A major theme of Sarte's political essays in the 1960s was of his disgust with the "*Americanization*" of the French working class who would much rather watch American TV shows dubbed into French than agitate for a revolution.

Sartre: With Fidel Castro and "Che" Guevara

Sartre visited Cuba in the 1960s to meet Fidel Castro and "Che" Guevara. After Guevara's death, Sartre declared him "*not only an intellectual but also the most complete human being of our age*" and the "*era's most perfect man*". He also complimented Guevara by professing that "*he lived his words, spoke his own actions and his story and the story of the world ran parallel*". He was, however, highly critical of the persecution of gays by Castro's regime, which he compared to Nazi persecution of the Jews, and said: "*In Cuba there are no Jews, but there are homosexuals*".

Sartre & Simone with Fidel Castro

Sartre & Simone with Che Guevara

During a collective hunger strike in 1974, Sartre visited Red Army Faction leader Andreas Baader in prison and criticized the harsh conditions of imprisonment.

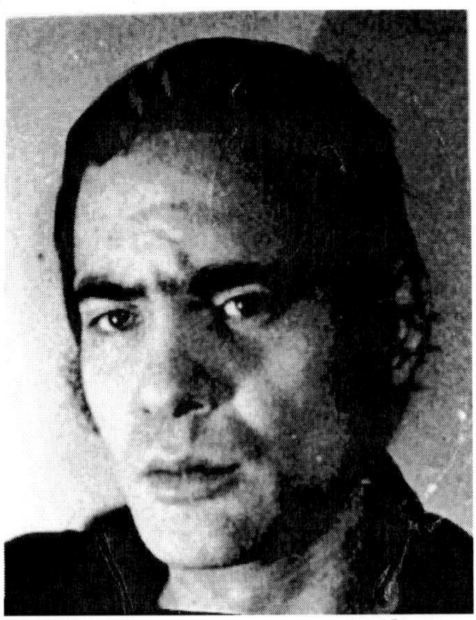

Andreas Baader

During his last years Sartre continued to speak out on political and social issues. In 1977, opposing the emerging trend of '*Eurocommunism*' independent of the Soviet Union, he accused the Italian Communist Party of collaborating with the Christian Democratic Party in a program of patronage and repression.

Towards the end of his life, Sartre became an anarchist. By the late 1960s Sartre had begun to support the Maoists, a movement that rejected the authority of established communist parties. However, despite aligning with the Maoists, Sartre said after the May events: "*If one rereads all my books, one will realize that I have not changed profoundly, and that I have always remained an anarchist.*" [50] He would later explicitly allow himself to be called an anarchist.

----

[50] Davis, Lydia; Auster, Paul; Contat, Michel; Sartre, Jean-Paul: "*Sartre at Seventy: An Interview by Jean-Paul Sartre and Michel Contat*". The New York Review of Books, 7 August, 1975.

Chapter 8

Existentialism: Jean-Paul Sartre

"We have spent two billion dollars on the greatest scientific gamble in history—and won."

--- Harry S. Truman, President of the United States, August 6, 1945, after the atom bomb was dropped on Hiroshima

Paris, 1945

"*Existentialism and Humanism*" is probably the most widely read of all Sartre's philosophical writings, and it is certainly one of his more accessible pieces. It was first presented as a public lecture at the Club Maintenant in Paris on 29 October 1945. It was a historical juncture. The World War II had just ended. Paris had been liberated from the Nazi Occupation and reprisals against collaborators were being meted out. The truth about the horrors of Auschwitz and Dachau was emerging. Just about two months' ago, on 6 and 9 August 1945, the *Little Boy* and *Fat Man* (atom bombs dropped by the USA) had landed on Hiroshima and Nagasaki killing more than 1, 70,000 people – exhibiting evidence of the human capacity for evil and destruction. In this backdrop, there was a felt-need for a re-examination of the previously unquestioned foundations of society and morality. Philosophical, and in particular moral, questions became increasingly relevant and were no longer of merely academic interest.

Existentialism

"Man is condemned to be free; because once thrown into the world, he is responsible for everything he does."

--- Jean-Paul Sartre, "Being and Nothingness"

The *Club Maintenant* lecture firmly linked Sartre's name with the philosophical movement known as existentialism. Only months before he had refused to accept the label: "*My philosophy is a philosophy of existence; I don't even know what Existentialism is*", he had asserted. As Simone de Beauvoir, Sartre's lifelong companion, records in her diary, "*Force of Circumstance*", neither she nor Sartre relished the term (which was first coined by Gabriel Marcel in 1943), but decided to go along with it: "*In the end, we took the epithet that everyone used for us and used it for our own purposes*".

But what precisely is existentialism? Sartre explicitly addressed this question in his lecture, describing existentialism as "*the least scandalous and the most austere*" [51] of teachings, and intended only for technicians and philosophers. Unlike material objects, like, a pen-knife crafted by a man for a definite purpose, for human beings "*existence comes before essence*". In other words, unlike objects created by a craftsman with a specific purpose, human beings have no predefined purpose or essence. Instead, they define themselves through their choices and actions. Sartre emphasized human freedom as a fundamental aspect of our existence. He believed that individuals are free to make choices and determine their paths in life. However, this freedom also comes with responsibility, as every choice carries consequences.

---

[51] Sartre, Jean-Paul. "*Existentialism Is a Humanism*". New Haven: Yale University Press, 2007.

Sartre was an atheist and did not believe in any Divine entity, like, God, in whose mind the 'essence' or purpose of our existence had been conceived. Nor did he unlike, say, Aristotle, believe in a common human nature which could be the source of morality. Sartre believed that human beings live in constant anguish, not solely because life is miserable, but because once born, we are *'condemned to be free'*. While the circumstances of our birth and upbringing are beyond our control, once we become self-aware (and we all do eventually), we have the freedom to make choices — choices that define our very *'essence'*. According to Sartre, there is no fixed design for how a human being should be and no God to give us a purpose. Therefore, the onus for defining ourselves, and by extension humanity, falls squarely on our shoulders. This lack of pre-defined purpose along with an 'absurd' existence that presents to us infinite choices is what Sartre attributes to the "*anguish of freedom*". With nothing to restrict us, we have the choice to take actions to become who we want to be and lead the life we want to live. Each choice we make defines us while at the same time revealing to us what we think a human being should be. And this incredible burden of responsibility that the free man has to bear is what relegates him to constant anguish.

Existentialism may be understood as the opposite of Descartes' philosophy of "*Cogito, ergo sum*" – '*I think, therefore I exist*', which was reversed and replaced by Kierkegaard as the maxim *'I exist, therefore I think'*. Rejecting the primacy of the rational, the ideal, Existentialism assigns primacy to decision, which often would be irrational. The very basis of Existentialism is that existence precedes essence, and that the-totality of existence is more than ideas or definitions of existence. Scottish theologian H. R. Mackintosh speaks of " *existential thinking" as "a mode of thought which concerns not the intellect merely but the whole personality of the man who awakens to it and adopts it. To think existentially, therefore, is to think not as a spectator of the ultimate issues of life and death, but as one who is committed to a decision upon them* " [52]

Good faith Vs. Bad faith

"Everything has been figured out, except how to live."

--- Jean-Paul Sartre

In the context of Jean-Paul Sartre's existentialist philosophy, "good faith" ('*bonne foi*') and "bad faith" ('*mauvaise fo*i') are two fundamental concepts that describe different ways in which individuals confront their own freedom and responsibility.

Sartre decried the idea of living without pursuing freedom. Denying all the possibilities of our freedom is acting in "*bad faith*", a phrase created by Sartre and discussed in '*Being and Nothingness*' (1943). Whenever we deny the endless possibilities in our lives, we deny the innate freedom we all have as human beings. To Sartre, this is essentially denying one's own humanity, and thus not an actor of "*good faith*". Sartre felt that cultural institutions attempt to define reality for us and that we must resist the temptation to let our reality be dictated by others.

Good faith, according to Sartre, refers to a state of being where individuals fully acknowledge and embrace their freedom and responsibility in making choices. It involves accepting the existential condition of uncertainty and the lack of predetermined meaning in life. In good faith, individuals recognize that they are the authors of their own actions and take ownership of the consequences that result from their choices.

---

[52] George, Munduvel V.: "*Existentialism and its· Message to Indian Thought Pattern*", pp. 68-69.

Bad faith, on the other hand, involves self-deception and a refusal to fully embrace one's freedom. It is a state in which individuals avoid taking full responsibility for their actions by denying their freedom or by pretending that they are not in control of their choices. According to Sartre, people who convince themselves that they have to do one particular kind of work or live in one particular city are living in bad faith. In '*Being and Nothingness*', he explains the concept of bad faith through the example of a waiter who is so immersed in his job that he considers himself to be first a waiter rather than a free human being. He is convinced that his present job is all that he can do, that it's all that he's meant to do, that he never considers the option of doing anything else in life. According to Sartre, we alone are responsible for everything that we really are, and by not exploring the myriad possibilities life presents to us we alone are responsible for restricting ourselves --- by restricting our freedom. "*We are left alone without an excuse*,"

Sartre and his fondness for Marxism

"Man lives in the midst of images. Literature offers him a critical image of himself."

— Jean-Paul Sartre, "Between Existentialism and Marxism"

An ardent believer in Marxism, Sartre was of the strong view that money restricts a person's freedom. The need of money, he reasoned, is the excuse people give themselves to shut down the idea of exploring other unconventional life choices. Capitalism, in his view, was the political system responsible for this phenomenon. He likened capitalism to a machine that traps people in a dragnet of working in jobs they don't like to induce them to buy things they don't need. According to him, this necessity of material things, to a great extent, did not exist in reality but rather was a man-made construct that led people to deny their freedom and refrain them from exploring other exciting options of life. Sartre was a vocal opponent of capitalism and took part in several Parisian protests in 1968 against the system. As a Marxist, he greatly admired Fidel Castro and Che Guevara, and for a considerable period of his life, was an admirer of the Soviet communist system.

Humanism

"*Man is not the sum of what he has already, but rather the sum of what he does not yet have, of what he could have.*"

--- Jean-Paul Sartre

Ultimately, Sartre was a humanist who wanted us to break free of our self-induced shackles and attain our fullest potential. He wanted us to be conscious of our freedom, and not to restrict ourselves by the popular definition of reality, so as to live life as we wished to live it. According to Sartre, "*We do not know what we want and yet we are responsible for what we are — that is the fact.*"

Sartre's humanism is intertwined with his emphasis on personal responsibility. Human beings, according to Sartre, are responsible for their actions and choices. This responsibility extends to the impact of one's actions on others and the ethical implications of those choices.

The humanism that Sartre endorses emphasises is the dignity of human beings; it stresses the centrality of human choice to the creation of all values. Sartre's existentialism captures the optimism usually associated with humanism. As an atheist, he advocates there is no God and, therefore, in the absence of any preestablished objective value, we alone are entirely responsible for what we become, and this puts the future of humanity in our own hands. Approvingly, therefore, Sartre quotes French essayist and poet Francis Ponge who said: "*Man is the future of man*" . [53]

----

[53] This emphasis on our 'freedom to choose' what we are is characteristic of all existentialist thinkers. Sartre was himself an atheist and advocated that there is no God. Some existentialists, including Gabriel Marcel, who were Christians, also, following on from the work of the nineteenth century Danish philosopher and theologian, Søren Kierkegaard, emphasise the need for doctrine to be derived from human experience and reject any appeal to eternal essence; and just like the atheist existentialists, they also believe that human beings are forced to create themselves.

Chapter 9
Frederich Nietzsche & Jean-Paul Sartre: A Comparative View

Sartre & Nietzsche: A Bird's Eye View

Jean-Paul Sartre (21 June 1905 – 15 April 1980) and Friedrich Wilhelm Nietzsche (15 October 1844 – 25 August 1900) were two influential philosophers who lived in different periods and developed distinct philosophical systems. While both had significant impacts on existentialism and postmodern thought, they held contrasting views on various fundamental concepts. Let's delve into a comparison of Sartre and Nietzsche in terms of their philosophical ideas and perspectives.

Nietzsche was a German philosopher, philologist, and composer whose work has exerted a profound influence on contemporary philosophy. Like Sartre, Nietzsche is also associated with existentialism that emphasizes individual existence, freedom, and responsibility. Though not typically categorized as an existentialist philosopher, Nietzsche had a profound influence on existential thought. Nietzsche's existentialism is often referred to as "existentialism before Sartre," as he delved into themes of individuality, the will to power, and the importance of self-overcoming. He critiqued traditional morality and embraced the idea of the "*Ubermensch*" [54] or "Overman," an individual who transcends conventional values and societal norms to create their

---

[54] This German word, '*Übermensch*', literally means "overman" and was coined in 1883 by the philosopher Friedrich Nietzsche. The Ubermensch was meant to be an ideal future human and an ultimate goal for humanity.

own moral code. Nietzsche rejected traditional beliefs in objective truths and saw the universe as inherently chaotic and amoral. Instead, he championed the idea of living authentically, embracing life's challenges.

Friedrich Nietzsche

The philosophy of Sartre, arguably the most prominent figure in the 20th-century existentialist movement, on the other hand, centres around the concept of "*existence precedes essence*," suggesting that we are not born with a predetermined purpose, and it is through our choices and actions that we create our own meanings in life. Sartre's emphasis on radical freedom and responsibility led him to claim that humans are "condemned to be free," implying that we are accountable for our choices even in the face of a seemingly indifferent and absurd world. [55]

Ethics & Morality

Nietzsche's views on morality diverged significantly from traditional ethical systems. He criticized the Christian notion of good and evil as a product of the "slave morality," which he believed was born out of resentment and weakness. Instead, Nietzsche championed the idea of "master morality," which is based on strength, power, and a re-evaluation of values. He encouraged individuals to embrace their desires and passions and to create their own moral standards.

Sartre's ethical framework, on the other hand, is grounded in his concept of radical freedom. Sartre also challenged conventional morality but approached it from a more atheistic standpoint. He argued that in a godless universe, there are no objective moral values or inherent meaning. This led him to conclude that individuals must actively choose their values and moral principles, even though it may lead to existential anguish and anxiety. Sartre's statement, "Man is condemned to be free," reflects his belief in the responsibility that comes with creating one's morality.

God and Nihilism

Nietzsche is often associated with the proclamation, "God is dead," which does not mean the literal death of God but the collapse of traditional religious beliefs and the loss of objective values. Nietzsche critiqued traditional morality, seeing it as a product of the weak, which suppresses human potential. He was critical of the

---

[55] Daigle, Christine: "*Sartre and Nietzsche: Brothers in arms*", Chapter 5 in 'Sartre's Second Century', edited by Benedict O'Donohoe and Roy Elveton, Cambridge Scholars Publishing, United Kingdom, 2009, pp. 56-72.

nihilistic tendencies arising from the death of God, as he believed it led to the denial of life's inherent value and the rejection of personal responsibility for creating meaningful existence

As regards Sartre, he was an atheist and believed that there is no inherent meaning or purpose in the universe. The absence of God leaves humanity without any external source of morality or guidance. This idea is encapsulated in his famous phrase, "Man is condemned to be free." For Sartre, the human condition is characterized by the anguish of having to choose in a world without absolute values, which leads to existential anxiety. Sartre's existentialism, though deeply concerned with the absurdity of life, does not fall into nihilism. He posited that even in an indifferent and absurd world, individuals have the power to find meaning through their choices and actions. While life may lack inherent meaning, Sartre believed that personal responsibility and authentic living could provide individuals with a sense of purpose.

The Role of the Individual

Both philosophers emphasized the importance of the individual in shaping their destiny and meaning in life. Nietzsche celebrated exceptional individuals who could rise above the herd mentality and traditional values to become the Ubermensch. He encouraged a life-affirming attitude that embraces challenges and struggles as opportunities for growth and self-actualization.

Sartre's notion of individuality is rooted in the idea of radical freedom. He believed that every individual has the power to shape their existence and is responsible for their choices. Sartre's existentialism promotes a form of humanism, where individuals are encouraged to create their own values and determine their destiny.

Art and Aesthetics

The two philosophers, Sartre and Nietzsche had distinct perspectives on art and aesthetics. Sartre believed that art is a means of capturing the human experience and providing insights into the human condition. He considered art as an expression of the artist's freedom and a reflection of their subjective world.

Nietzsche also recognized the significance of art and creativity. He saw art as a way to affirm life and unleash the "Dionysian forces" [56] within individuals, embracing the primal and irrational aspects of existence. Nietzsche celebrated the role of the artist as a creator and praised artistic expression as a means of transcending the limitations of mundane existence.

In conclusion, Sartre and Nietzsche both were influential philosophers who made profound contributions to existentialism and postmodern thought. While Sartre emphasized individual freedom and responsibility in a world devoid of inherent meaning, Nietzsche rejected traditional moralities and sought the affirmation of life's complexities and the re-evaluation of values. Despite their differences, both philosophers encouraged individuals to embrace their authentic selves and create meaning in a seemingly

---

[56] "*Dionysian forces*" typically refers to the concept of Dionysian energy or impulses, which are associated with the Greek god Dionysus. In ancient Greek mythology and philosophy, Dionysus was the god of wine, fertility, and revelry, among other things. His worship and rituals were characterized by ecstatic and uninhibited celebrations, often involving music, dance, and wine.

Nietzsche expanded on the idea of Dionysian forces in his work "*The Birth of Tragedy*." He contrasted the Apollonian and Dionysian principles as two fundamental artistic drives. The Apollonian represents order, rationality, and form, while the Dionysian represents chaos, emotions, and instinctual drives. Nietzsche saw the combination of both elements as essential for the creation of great art and the understanding of human existence.

n broader terms, "Dionysian forces" can refer to the primordial and instinctual aspects of human nature, which often involve spontaneous and wild emotions, creativity, and a connection to the irrational and mysterious elements of life.

All forms of enthusiasm and ecstasy are Dionysian. Music is the most Dionysian of the arts, since it appeals directly to man's instinctive, chaotic emotions and not to his formally reasoning mind.

meaningless world. Their works, therefore, continue to be influential and relevant to this day in contemporary discussions about the nature of human existence.

Chapter 10

"Hell is other people": Sartre on Personal Relationships

"There's no need for red-hot pokers. Hell is other people."

- Jean-Paul Sartre, "No Exit"

"*Hell is other people*!" [57] is a famous line from '*No Exit*' (1944), a philosophical play by Sartre. In *No Exit*, the essential argument is that human relationships are basically fraught with conflict. This resembles Sartre's view, in *Being and Nothingness*, his most famous philosophical work, that "*conflict is the original meaning of being-for-others*", a view whose significance and implications are debatable.

There are views arguing that both statements reflect a pessimistic view of Sartre that interpersonal relations are conflictual and full of misunderstandings, struggles, and attempts at controlling the Other. There are, however, many others who argue that Sartre's intent is not to insert an unbearable pessimism into the heart of human relations, but rather to show how bad faith, which occurs when consciousness lies to and deceives itself, can negatively affect our interpersonal and social relations. They also argue that any turning toward authenticity could mitigate the problems and conflicts whose concealed origin is our attempt at escaping or negating our radical freedom. Such views take Sartre's

[57] Sartre, Jean-Paul: "*No Exit and Three Other Plays*", Vintage, New York, 1989, p.45.

"*existence precedes essence*" and his notions of freedom, condemnation, and the situation as the ground from which any attempt at escaping bad faith should arise.

'No Exit': The Plot

"[...] a phenomenon of the modern theatre – played all over the continent already. It should be seen whether you like it or not."

--- Stark Young, American playwright, novelist & literary critic, The New York Reporter

'*No Exit*' opens with its three damned souls — Joseph Garcin, Inèz Serrano, and Estelle Rigault, —led into an old-fashioned room in Hell and locked inside by a mysterious valet. They are complete strangers, do not know one other, but they do know that they are dead and now in hell. They had all expected torture devices ready to punish them for eternity, but instead, find a plain room furnished in the style of the French 'Second Empire' [58]. In this room, distractions are impossible because the three strangers cannot blink, sleep, or dream and because there are no windows, books, or mirrors.

Since there are no mirrors in this room, the three strangers cannot see either themselves or how each one is seen by the Others.

[58] The Second French Empire was the 18-year Imperial Bonapartist regime of Napoleon III from 14 January 1852 to 27 October 1870. In its early years (1852–59), the empire was authoritarian but enjoyed economic growth and pursued a favourable foreign policy.

Stark Young Critic, New York Reporter

At first, none of the souls will admit the reason for their damnation: Garcin says that he was executed for being an outspoken pacifist, while Estelle insists that a mistake has been made in her case; Inèz, however, is the only one to demand that they all stop lying to themselves and confess to their moral crimes. She refuses to believe that they have all ended up in the room by accident. Soon they begin to torture and torment themselves by criticizing and reproaching one another whilst attempting to justify and explain their actions and deeds in the lives they have lived; and soon, as they get on one another's nerves, Inez realizes their situation: "*Each of us will act as torturer of the two others.*" [59]

[59] Sartre, Jean-Paul: "*No Exit and Three Other Plays*", Vintage, New York, 1989, p.17.

Garcin suggests that they try to leave themselves alone and to be silent, but Inèz starts talking about execution and Estelle vainly wants to find a mirror to check on her appearance. Inèz tries to seduce Estelle by offering to be her "mirror" by telling her everything she sees but ends up frightening her instead. Soon it becomes clear that Inèz is attracted to Estelle, Estelle is attracted to Garcin, and Garcin is not attracted to either of the two women.

After a spell of argument, they all decide to confess their crimes so they know what to expect from one other. Garcin admits he cheated on and mistreated his wife, and was executed by firing squad for desertion. Inèz is a manipulative sadist who seduced her cousin's wife, Florence, and convinced her to leave her husband; the cousin was later hit and killed by a tram and Florence asphyxiated herself and Inèz by flooding the room with gas while they slept. As for Estelle, she had an affair and then killed their child, as a result of which the child's father committed suicide. Even after their revelations, they continue to get on one another's nerves.

Garcin finally starts giving in to Estelle's attempts to seduce him, which drives Inèz crazy. Garcin is, however, constantly burdened by his own guilt, and begs Estelle to tell him he is not a coward for deserting his country during wartime. While she complies, Inèz mockingly tells him that Estelle is just feigning love to him so that she can be with a man—any man.

The constant mockery and sarcasm by Inèz provoke Garcin to attempt an abrupt escape. As he tries to open the door, it inexplicably and suddenly opens, but he is unable to leave, and the others remain as well. He wants to convince Inèz that he is not cowardly, but she refuses, saying that he is obviously a coward, and keeps on making him miserable.

Tormented to the core, shortly before the end of the play, Garcin realizes and declares what the whole is all about from the very beginning: "*There's no need for red-hot pokers. Hell is other people.*"

Estelle, on her part, tries to persevere in her seduction of Garcin, but he tells her that he cannot make love while Inèz is watching. Estelle, infuriated, picks up a paper knife and repeatedly stabs Inèz. Inèz simply mocks Estelle, reminding her that they are all already dead. As Estelle begins to laugh hysterically at the idea of them being dead and trapped together forever, the others join her in a prolonged fit of laughter as Garcin finally concludes, "*Eh bien, continuons...*" ("Well then, let's get on with it...").

The Others

The power of "*the others*" and their gaze is the main idea of Sartre's play '*No Exit*'. Sartre experienced this first hand in Nazi-occupied France, as Nazi soldiers were ever-present and watchful. French citizens were always made aware of their powerlessness as long as they were being observed. This inspired Sartre to use the phrase "the others".

Humans are social creatures and seek validation from others. These moments occur in the play when Inèz offers to be a mirror for Estelle, or Garcin insists his vindication must come from Inèz. While this validation can be helpful, it can also be harmful.

Inèz represents the worst of the gaze and the power of "the others". She uses her presence and gaze to control the other two characters. However, she too is not immune to "the others". The romance between Garcin and Estelle together is her torture, and the mere possibility of them touching each other is painful and inescapable for her.

Estelle welcomes Garcin's gaze. Estelle's past life was dominated by her desire to be validated by other men. Her femininity is important to her, and she constantly thinks about how she appears to others.

Being and Nothingness

"I exist, that is all, and I find it nauseating."

— Jean-Paul Sartre, "Being and Nothingness"

In his more philosophical work '*Being and Nothingness*', Sartre paints a bleak picture of human relationships. [60] He says that relationships involve a constant struggle over freedom, which is the only thing that really matters. [61] This tension arises because we either treat other people as objects, which undermines their freedom, or we allow ourselves to be treated as objects by them, which undermines ours. Either way, someone's freedom is threatened, so encountering another person necessarily results in a struggle for dominance. Thus, Sartre's pessimistic view of relationships seems to be grounded in his broader philosophy.

Misinterpretation

While *Being and Nothingness* seems to support the popular interpretation of *No Exit*, according to which

---

[60] Sartre discusses relationships in Chapter 3 ("Concrete Relations with Others") of Part 3 ("Being-for-Others").

[61] Sartre discusses freedom in Chapter 1 ("Being and Doing: Freedom") or Part 4 ("Having, Doing, and Being").

relationships are always bad, this interpretation, many critics, such as Kiki Berk, argue [62], is mistaken. In an oral preface for a 1964 recording of the play, Sartre claims that his statement "*hell is other people*" has been commonly misunderstood. In his words:

> "*It has been thought that what I meant by that was that our relations with other people are always poisoned, that they are invariably hellish relations. But what I really mean is something totally different. I mean that if relations with someone else are twisted, vitiated [i.e., corrupted], then that other person can only be hell.*" [63]

In other words, according to Sartre, the statement "*hell is other people*" is implicitly conditional. What it means is other people are hell for us only if our relationships with them are bad. He explains further:

> "*If my relations are bad, I am situating myself in a total dependence on someone else. And then I am indeed in hell. And there are a vast number of people in the world who are in hell because they are too dependent on the judgment of other people. But that does not at all mean that one cannot have relations with other people. It simply brings out the capital importance of all other people for each one of us.*" [64]

---

[62] Berk, Kiki: ""*Hell Is Other People": Sartre on Personal Relationships*", 1000-Word Philosophy, 8 February, 2021.

[63] Sartre, Jean-Paul, 1976. "*Sartre on Theater*". Michel Contat and Michel Rybalka (eds). London: Random House, 1976, p.199.

[64] Sartre, Jean-Paul, 1976. "*Sartre on Theater*". Michel Contat and Michel Rybalka (eds). London: Random House, 1976, p.199-200.

According to Sartre, other people's judgments invariably enter into our thoughts and feelings about ourselves. This isn't bad as such, for these judgements help us to have a true knowledge of ourselves. What's bad is when we allow ourselves (like Garcin) to become overly dependent on the opinions of other people. This leads to those people being "hell" for us. But although other people can be hell for us if we relate to them in this way, they needn't be if we don't.

Radical Conversion & Authentic Living

How does this conditional reading of "*hell is other people*" fit with Sartre's pessimistic account of relationships in *Being and Nothingness*? The key to answering this question lies in a footnote at the end of his discussion of human relationships:

> *"These considerations do not exclude the possibility of an ethics of deliverance and salvation. But this can be achieved only after a radical conversion which we cannot discuss here."* [65]

In the context of Sartre's existentialist philosophy, "radical conversion" refers to a transformative process in which an individual undergoes a profound change in their way of being, thinking, and living. It involves a fundamental shift in one's consciousness and understanding of the world, leading to a new mode of existence and engagement with reality.

The "radical conversion" to which Sartre refers is a transformation from "bad faith" to authenticity, which is at the very core of Sartre's existentialist philosophy. For Sartre,

---

65 Sartre, Jean-Paul: "*Being and Nothingness*". London: Routledge, 1958, p.412.

authentic living was about finding meaning in the projects we undertake and our encounters with others.[66] People are in bad faith when they deceive themselves into thinking they aren't ultimately free and responsible for their actions. Making excuses for what one does, inaccurately labelling oneself, inventing a role in order to hide behind it (as Garcin does)—these are all ways of being in bad faith. [67] Relationships between people who are in bad faith are bound to fail; relationships between people who are authentic, on the other hand, can well succeed.

Heaven is Each Other

Unfortunately, Sartre never tells us what it takes to undergo this "radical conversion" from bad faith to authenticity. All he tells us is that he will tackle this problem in a later work, which he began but never finished. [68] But he did continue to think about relationships. In a 1971 interview, when asked about his statement that "hell is other people," he responds:

> *"But that's only that side of the coin. The other side, which no one seems to mention, is also "Heaven is each other." ... Hell is separateness, uncommunicability, self-centeredness, lust for power, for riches, for fame.*

---

66 Ang, J. M. (2019): "*Can existentialists be happy? Authentic life, authentic happiness*", Science, Religion and Culture, Vol. 6 No.1, pp. 122–129.

67 Sartre discusses bad faith in Chapter 2 ("Bad Faith") or Part 1 ("The Problem of Nothingness").

68 Sartre, Jean-Paul: "*Notebooks for an Ethics*". Chicago: University of Chicago Press, 1992.

> *Heaven, on the other hand, is very simple—and very hard: caring about your fellow beings*." [69]

So, even late in his life, Sartre was of the view that relationships can succeed. [70]

----

[69] Gerassi, John: "*Talking with Sartre: Conversations and Debates*". New Haven: Yale University Press, 2009, p.130.
[70] Ibid., 56.

Chapter 11

Sartreism: Through the lens of Critics

"I am. I am, I exist, I think, therefore I am; I am because I think, why do I think? I don't want to think any more, I am because I think that I don't want to be, I think that I . . . because . . . ugh!"

-Jean-Paul Sartre, 'Nausea'

How original was Sartre as a thinker?

Sartre's philosophy, even the word "*existentialism*", which Sartre popularised from 1946, came from other philosophers. Soren Kierkegaard, an early 19th century Danish philosopher, theologian and poet, is widely considered the first existentialist philosopher, though he did not use the term 'existentialism'. He proposed that each individual—not society or religion—is solely responsible for giving meaning to life and living it passionately and "authentically".

Kierkegaard was influenced by Schelling (1775-1854), whose lectures he attended at Berlin. He was also a good student of Greek Philosophy and Hegelian Idealism. He had a very high respect of Socrates and the Socratic Method. He was sent by his father Michael J. Kierkegaard, a rich wool merchant, to be trained for the ministry. But his primary interest being in philosophy, although he completed his theological studies, he was never ordained. The breaking of his engagement with Regine Olsen in 1841, in spite of his ardent love for her, caused in him a deep change in mental attitude. *'Before God we are always in the wrong'*, he used to insist. Being very critical of the State Church in Denmark, he believed his mission to be to *'introduce Christianity into Christendom'.* As he continued to be unpopular till his death, he made no income from his books. Having fainted on the side of a public road, he died in a hospital. When asked, whether he wanted to receive the Sacrament, he replied, *'Yes, but not from a priest'*. There was a hubbub even about his burial, because he was a pungent critic of the established church.

By common consent Kierkegaard is the father of modern Existentialism. This line of thinking is traceable in the writings of St. Augustine, Pascal, Nietzsche, Dostoevsky, and others.

Soren Kierkegaard

The term “existentialist” was coined by the French Catholic philosopher Gabriel Marcel in the mid-1940s. At first, when Marcel applied the term at a colloquium in 1945, Sartre rejected it. Sartre subsequently changed his mind and, on October 29, 1945, publicly adopted the existentialist label in a lecture published later as a short book titled *“L'existentialismeest un humanisme” (Existentialism is a Humanism)* that did much to popularize existentialist thought.

Gabriel Marcel

Though he was not the first to propose the idea, Sartre was indisputably the most articulate spokesperson of "*existentialism*" and was at the vanguard of the movement to make it universally popular, particularly during the post-war period. But "*Existentialism*" is in no way his brainchild; and critics, therefore, resent for he is sometimes mistakenly credited as its originator.

Sartre's Existentialist Marxism: A bit of an Oxymoron

It is difficult to see what Sartre "believed" for his thinking shifted all the time. The single, consistent strand in Sartre's philosophy is his glorification of the individual. But there is a glaring contradiction, his critics argue, between his existentialist philosophy of individual 'freedom' and the Marxist doctrine that he embraced.

Sartre attempted to synthesise the two in his "*Critique de la raison dialectique" ("Critique of Dialectical Reason"), which he* *published in 1960.*The second volume of the *Critique* was drafted in 1958 and published in France in 1985.

Sarte's Rejoinder: "Critique of Dialectical Reason"

In "*Critique de la raison dialectique"("Critique of Dialectical Reason"), Sartre* was strongly influenced by his friend and associate Maurice Merleau-Ponty, whose writings in the late 1940s and early 1950s (such as, "*Sense and Non-sense"*) were pioneering a path towards a synthesis of existentialism and Marxism.

'Critique of Dialectical Reason' was written at a time when Sartre no longer identified Marxism with the Soviet Union or French Communism. In *Critique,* Sartre puts forward a revision of his earlier philosophy of existentialism and recognizes more fully than before the effect of historical and material conditions on individual and collective choice. He interprets Marxism as a contemporary philosophy *par excellence.*

"*Critique*" did not receive the attention it deserved as it came out in the early 1960's when the intellectual hegemony of existentialism – virtually universal in the post-war years – was giving way to a new intellectual passion called "post-*structuralism*". Nonetheless, philosophers and scholars have been keen to assess where it stands in relation to Sartre's earlier seminal work, "*Being and Nothingness".*

The reaction has been mixed. Scholars like George Kline and Fredric Jameson see the work as essentially a repudiation of Sartre's earlier existentialist stance. Hazel Barnes and Peter Caws, on the other hand, see a shift in emphasis between the two works but not a difference of kind. Polish Philosopher and historian of ideas, Leszek Kolakowski is of the view that *Critique* represents an abandonment of Sartre's original existentialism and it absurdly depicts Marxism as *"invincible"*.

Chapter 12

Sartre: Between Existentialism and Marxism

"The majority of the proletariat ... forms a closed society with no doors or windows.* [There is] *only one way in, and a very narrow one—the Communist Party"

-- Jean-Paul Sartre

In his "*Critique de la raison dialectique*" ("Critique of Dialectical Reason"), published in 1960, Sartre attempted to synthesise his existentialist philosophy of individual 'freedom' and the Marxist doctrine that he embraced, which was gaining much attention and interest, particularly among the masses, following the historic October revolution in Russia in 1917. A reconciliation between the two philosophies had become necessary as Sartre, in his political activities since 1941, was visibly aligning himself with the left that espoused the Marxist doctrine. But then there was an apparent fundamental conflict between the two, namely, Sartre's original brand of Existentialism that advocated individual freedom, and the philosophy of 'Marxism' founded on collective action. Naturally, therefore, there was confusion and controversy galore and it called for some reconciliation of these two strands of thought and Sartre sought to do it through his "*Critique of Dialectical Reason*" published in 1960. For a fair appreciation of his work, which is more in the nature of a rejoinder to set at rest many of the questions his pollical activities of earlier nearly two decades had given rise to, it is necessary to go through the historical course of evolution of these two philosophies, Existentialism and Marxism, to which we may now turn.

Between Existentialism and Marxism

Existentialism and Marxism have arguably been the most widely discussed and widely held philosophies of the twentieth century. The first was dominant in Western Europe and was also popular in the United States, while the second came to be not only the official doctrine of all communist countries but, in one form or another, has been accepted as a guide for many movements and parties throughout the world.

Since the beginning of the Second World War and for over 20 years thereafter, the proponents of these two schools of thought remained engaged in continual debate with one another. The centre of this controversy was France. There the principal spokesperson in favour of existentialism was Jean-Paul Sartre and his associates, who developed their positions in direct contact and contest with Marxism. They lived in a continent where, unlike in thc United States, socialism had influenced public life for almost a century, while at the same time the Communist Party, followed by most of the working class, would get a quarter of the vote, and exert heavy pressure upon radical intellectuals. These circumstances compelled the proponents of the left to make clear their attitude toward Marxism at every stage in the evolution of their views.

In this backdrop, Sartre's philosophical stance did undergo change over time and his evolution as such was rather paradoxical. To begin with, he worked out his original existentialist ideas under the sway of nonmaterialist thinkers such as Edmund Husserl and Martin Heidegger as a deliberate challenge to Marxism. In "*Being and Nothingness*" (1943) and "*Materialism and Revolution*" (1947), Sartre presented his philosophy as an alternative to dialectical materialism. Then in the late 1950s he made a turnabout and embraced Marxism, at least in words—which for him, as he explained in the first volume of his autobiography, "*Les Mots*" ('The Words, 1964) had a reality greater than the objective world.

In 1960, Sartre published his philosophical treatise, "*The Critique of Dialectical Reason*", the first section of which was brought out in English as "*Search for a Method*", Sartre observed that "*existentialism has become a subordinate branch of Marxism which aspires to renew and enrich it*". Thus the phenomenologist of existence who condemned dialectical materialism as false and a foe to human freedom in the 1940s seemingly proposed to marry Marxism and existentialism. [71]

Sartre's Philosophy: Evolution

While working as a teacher in the 1930s, Sartre's brand of existentialism took shape. Throughout this period, he lived in hotel rooms and worked out of cafes and bars. It was an existence marked by its freedom from the kinds of constraints faced by most ordinary people—the day-to-day drudgery of working life, the family responsibilities, worries about mortgage payments, bills and so on. He was virtually detached from the world, which could lead one to make the kind of abstract statements of existential angst that Sartre is famous for. "*Every existing thing is born without reason, prolongs itself out of weakness, and dies by chance*", reflects the protagonist in Sartre's maiden philosophical novel *Nausea*, published in 1938.

According to Sartre, the Second World War was the defining event of his life. "*That was when*", he later wrote, "*I made the*

---

[71] In 1974, Sartre's book titled "*Between Existentialism and Marxism*, was originally published. This book presents a full decade of Sartre's work, from the publication of the '*Critique of Dialectical Reason*' in 1960, the basic philosophical turning-point in his post-war development, to the inception of his major study on Flaubert, the first volumes of which appeared in 1971. The essays and interviews collected here form a vivid panorama of the range and unity of Sartre's interests, since his deliberate attempt to wed his original existentialism to a rethought Marxism. [See: Sartre, Jean-Paul: "*Between Existentialism and Marxism*": Set 3 (Radical Thinkers), Translated by John Mathews, Verso Books, 17 January 2008.]

transition from individualism and the pure individual ... to the social, to socialism". Sartre was conscripted in late 1939 and was put to work in a meteorological unit near the front line between France and Germany. In his notebooks from this period, we can see the tensions playing out between his existentialist standpoint and the highly constraining circumstances of the army. His initial understanding was that, individuals were free to accept or reject the war— and it was happening because of each individual's choice not to oppose it. So, in his notebook, he reflected: "*The further I go, the more I see that men deserve war ... The declaration of war, which was the fault of certain men, we all adopt as our own, with our freedom*". The real world was so different from the abstract world he lived in earlier --- it was time for him to understand.

"Being and Nothingness" (1943): *Sartre rolls out his brand of Existentialism*

In his notebooks, Sartre first set-out the core ideas of his masterwork '*Being and Nothingness*' published in 1943. The basic insight of Sartre's existentialism is, as we have discussed earlier, that "*existence precedes essence*". We are, as individuals, thrown into a world. To begin with, we exist. Only subsequently do we come to find meaning in our lives. "*Man*", as Sartre put it, "*is nothing else but that which he makes of himself*". To live authentically, one must not shy away from the absolute, anguish-inducing freedom inherent to existence. Therefore, one must recognise that whatever situation we are in, the way we choose to act is up to us alone. It means that we should strive at every point to "*be ourselves*!" and not let other people or circumstances define who we are.

1941: Sartre released from a German POW camp and returns to Paris

Released from a German prisoner of war camp in early 1941, Sartre returned to Paris, and immediately set about the work of organising resistance, of a sort, to the Nazi occupation. This was sought to be done through the "*Socialism and Freedom*" group—comprising Sartre and a number of his close intellectual associates, as well as various figures from the anti-Stalinist left. It was a sign of a shift in his understanding of the role of the intellectual in society. He would no longer keep himself confined to the role of an intellectual as an 'outsider', not associated with the day-to-day struggles of the world. The basic questions raised by the war—as to how the individual could be "free" in the event of an enemy occupation stared in the face or, more generally, how our fundamental autonomy as individuals could be recognised in the face of the constraints imposed on us by history and society.

Sartre's engagement with such questions led him to put a more activist spin on his existentialism. Freedom, he realized, could not simply remain reduced to an abstract condition. Rather, he began to see and emphasize that our individual existence was linked to the fate of society as a whole, and that a genuinely 'liberatory' philosophy was needed to address the question of how the conditions for individual freedom could be ensured at this level. And this began to be reflected in his post-war works by way of addition of a kind of existential version of the Enlightenment philosopher Immanuel Kant's '*categorical imperative*'[72]. Whereas

[72] Kant defines 'categorical imperatives' as commands or moral laws all persons must follow, regardless of their desires or extenuating circumstances. As morals, these imperatives are binding on everyone. To illustrate the categorical imperative, Kant uses four examples that cover the range of morally significant situations which arise. These examples include committing suicide, making false promises, failing to develop one's abilities, and refusing to be charitable. [Source: Muscente, Kailee Kodama: "*Categorical Imperatives and the Case for Deception: Part I*", Teachers College, Columbia University, July 13, 2020.]

the stress in '*Being and Nothingness*' had been on the essential conflict involved in our relationship with others, epitomised by the most famous of all Sartrean tropes, "*hell is -- other people*"—by the end of the war, he had come to a different conclusion: "*I cannot make liberty my aim unless I make that of others equally my aim*".

29 October 1945: "Existentialism is a humanism": Sartre's lecture at Club Maintenant in Paris

In October 1945, Sartre launched the journal "*Les Temps Modernes*" ('Modern Times'), which he edited along with de Beauvoir and a number of his other close friends such as Raymond Aron and Maurice Merleau-Ponty. Finally, there were his lectures—the most famous of which was delivered at Club Maintenant in Paris, on 29 October 1945, titled "*Existentialism is a humanism*". The excitement about Sartre was by this point so intense that the crowd for this lecture overflowed the venue, and there was an occasion when the crowd was so huge that a number of people fainted.

It was a historic juncture. Revolution was very much in the air throughout France. And the alternatives offered in the political mainstream were far from satisfying. The French Communist Party (the PCF) returned to the "popular front" strategy of the pre-war years—reflecting Stalin's desire not to upset the applecart following his agreement on the post-war division of Europe with British Prime Minister Winston Churchill and US President Franklin Roosevelt. On the right it was the same old conservatism—a return to family values, order, respectability and so on.

Given this ambience, there was a widespread yearning for freedom, particularly among young people—but little sense of the politics that could make it a reality. Existentialism seemed, for a while, to hold out the hope of a new beginning, although the time demanded Sartre to re-position himself to conform to the new realities, which he did. Reflecting back on this period he later said: "*For my part, I had become a convinced socialist ... but an anti-hierarchical and libertarian one, one in favour of direct democracy*". In 1948, Sartre and several other prominent figures in the anti-Stalinist left established the *Revolutionary Democratic Assembly* (RDR). In its founding statement, they wrote:

> "*Between the rottenness of capitalist democracy, the weaknesses and defects of a certain social democracy and the limitation of Communism to its Stalinist form, we believe an assembly of free men for revolutionary democracy is capable of giving new life to the principles of freedom and human dignity by binding them to the struggle for social revolution.*"

Unfortunately, the whole thing collapsed in a heap barely a year later, with membership never having exceeded 4,000 at most. The cause of its break-up was the lack of any coherent political analysis that could withstand the immense pressures of the emerging Cold War. The lesson Sartre drew from the shipwreck of the RDR was that the anti-Stalinist left couldn't really offer a genuine alternative. The key to the future was the working class. And this class was by and large under the sway of the PCF. As Sartre himself put it: "*The majority of the proletariat ... forms a closed society with no doors or windows.* [There is] *only one way in, and a very narrow one—the Communist Party*".

From around 1952 until 1956, Sartre became a kind of "*fellow traveller*" of the PCF. In his book "*The Communists and Peace*", he stated his "*agreement with the Communists on specific and limited subjects, arguing on the basis of my principles and not theirs*". What is clear, however, is that over time he began to adapt his principles somewhat to fit more into the PCF mould.

The most appalling situation came with Sartre's visit to the USSR in 1954. On his return, he published a series of articles lauding the supposedly open culture, freedom of speech and so on. Perhaps even more appallingly, Sartre later tried to save the grace by claiming that owing to his ill-health, his secretary did a chunk of the work on these articles on his behalf.

Nevertheless, Sartre's position during this time wasn't quite like he was an outright apologist for Stalinism. While he adapted himself to the PCF in some ways, in others he maintained a more independent stance. So, while *Les Temps Modernes* continued to provide a platform for contributions from the anti-Stalinist left, Sartre also continued to publish works in his own name that went strongly against the grain of Communist policy.

Critique of Dialectical Reason

The contradictory nature of Sartre's politics found its most worked out philosophical expression in his monumental "*Critique of Dialectical Reason*", published in 1960. The Critique was an attempt to rejuvenate what Sartre saw as the genuine, critical spirit of Marxism, using insights drawn from existentialism. "*If we do not wish the dialectic to become a divine law again*", he wrote, "*it must proceed from individuals and not from some kind of supra-individual ensemble*". What he ended up with, however, according to critics, was neither existentialism nor Marxism, but a fundamentally flawed mix-up of ideas and concepts drawn from each. Sartre was of the view that the Stalinist distortions of Marxism (namely, dialectic as "*a divine law*", the individual sacrificed to the "*supra-individual ensemble*" and so on), were the results a defect in Marxism itself. In his effort to reconcile the two, he apparently, if not unwittingly, ended up by kind of rationalising Stalin's action. The cure was worse than the disease. What, the critics say, was required to save Marxism wasn't the addition of existentialist philosophy, but rather a return to the genuine Marxist tradition—the tradition of Marx and Engels themselves, and of later figures such as Vladimir Lenin, Rosa Luxemburg, Leon Trotsky and Georg Lukács. In this tradition, in contrast to Stalinism, the notion of individual freedom was very much centred. The struggle for socialism, as Marx put it in the Communist Manifesto, is a struggle for a society "*in which the free development of each is the condition for the free development of all*".

So how are we to assess Sartre's evolution and work overall as a philosopher? Well!, while neither his original "pure" existentialism nor his later existentialist brand of Marxism is beyond criticism, his status as among the most committed left-wing public intellectuals of the twentieth century is certainly worth celebrating. His consistent radicalism and activist orientation in the post-war period decidedly place him far above most of today's intellectuals.

Are existentialism and Marxism compatible?

But the important question that still remains is: Are existentialism and Marxism compatible? To what extent, if any, can these philosophies be conjoined? Can they really be synthesised into a coherent unit?

In a seminal paper entitled "*Marxism Versus Existentialism*", George Novack explores these questions and conclude that the contending world outlooks cannot be harmonised or integrated into one containing "the best features" of both. He likens the effort to reconcile the two to that of a legendary alchemist who thought that by putting together fire and water he would concoct that most desirable of delights, "*fire-water*". Actually, one nullifies or extinguishes the other when they come into contact. According to Novack, it is the same with Marxism and existentialism. Their fundamental positions over a broad spectrum of problems extending from philosophy and sociology to morality and politics are so divergent that they cannot really be reconciled.

Like Novack, most interpreters and adherents of existentialism, especially the theists among them, are of the view that the two are not reconcilable. They reject Marxism totally because it fails to recognise what to them is the most meaningful aspect of being: the sovereign subjectivity and dignity of the individual. They maintain that materialist theory debases people to mere objects while socialist practice stamps out personal freedom. Orthodox Marxists, on the other hand, no less firmly insist that the contending philosophies have far too many principled differences to be welded into one.

In between stand a variegated group who agree with Sartre that the two can be fused into onc that will reinforce both. In the United States the noted psychoanalytical sociologist Erich Fromm is the most ardent champion of the thesis that existentialism and Marxism are substantially identical. According to Fromm's concept of Marx, based on Marx's "*Concept of Man*" (1961), Marx's thinking is humanist existentialism. The doctrines appear alike to him since both protest against the alienation in modern society and seek ways to overcome it. "*Marx's philosophy*", he writes, "*constitutes a spiritual existentialism in secular language and because of this spiritual quality is opposed to the materialistic practice and thinly disguised materialistic philosophy of our age. Marx's aim, socialism, based on his theory of man, is essentially prophetic Messianism in the language of the 19th century.*"

This transmutation of the materialist Marx into a precursor and preacher of existentialism is typical of radical humanists of very different backgrounds and beliefs; Fromm is their chief American mouthpiece. They locate the "true" Marx in the early "*Economic and Philosophic Manuscripts of 1844*", also referred to as the '*Paris*

Manuscripts' ('*Pariser Manuskripte*'), which mark transitional stages of his development, instead of in the ripe conclusions of his mature thoughts. They contend that Marx has been misrepresented as a crude dialectical materialist by his orthodox disciples from Engels to Lenin—until the radical humanists revealed that he really was an ethical existentialist.

Fromm's reconciliation of dialectical materialism with existentialism is as ill-founded as his astonishing statement that "*Marx's atheism is the most advanced form of rational mysticism*". The atheistic Marx is no more a mystic than the Marx of scientific socialism is an existentialist.

Sartrean existentialism, critics argue, is another attempt to eke out the real or alleged deficiencies of Marxist thought. But it is, on its part, equally unlikely to be more successful than its predecessors. The existentialists stress that the individual's sincerest act and tragic responsibility is the necessity to choose between anguishing alternatives and take the consequences. Sartre shrinks from doing this in philosophy. The confrontation of existentialism with dialectical materialism is a genuine case of "either-or." But Sartre wants to embrace both Kierkegaard and Marx without choosing between them. The trouble, however, is that dialectical materialism and existentialism are contrary-minded and oriented along diametrically different lines. They clash at almost every point on the major issues of philosophy, sociology, morality, and politics. It is a pointless task to try to mate these opposites. In the words of Novack:

> *"The first commandment of existentialism is, as has been said: "Be yourself!" This is not a bad maxim, and it ought to be applied as strictly to philosophies as to personalities. Let existentialism be what it really is—the ideological end product of liberalism and individualism—and not pretend to be something else. Let Marxism likewise be what it should be: that dialectical materialism which is*

the scientific expression and practical guide of the world socialist revolution of the working masses."

Therefore, let not the two be intermixed and confused. Their mismating can produce only stillborn offspring, whether in philosophy or in politics.

Chapter 13

Was Sartre a Marxist?

"Ever since Marx, philosophy must lead to action. Otherwise it is irrelevant. . . . Philosophers must be angry, and, in this world, stay angry."

--Jean-Paul Sartre (1972) [73]

"An anti-Communist is a dog": Sartre [74]

After he was convinced, particularly after his return to Paris in 1941, after having served a stint in the army as a meteorologist, including a spell in the German prisoner of war camp, that engagement with abstract intellectual questions of individual freedom as an 'outsider would not really help much, Sartre decided not stay away from active politics and political developments round the world. And he remained so ever thereafter.

It was an unusual time. In the wake of the Second World War, the politics round the world was constantly undergoing changes. The changing configuration of politics both at home and abroad naturally impacted on Sartre's philosophical stance as well. Thus, while he was writing the *Critique*, he was also involved in the campaign against France's war in Algeria (1954-62). This again put him at odds with the PCF, which in 1956 gave its support to new powers demanded by the recently elected French Socialist Party. The PCF's stance, along with the crushing of the Hungarian

[73] Ibid., 62, 178. The quote is from a conversation that took place in April, 1972.
[74] Aronson, Ronald: "*Camus and Sartre: The Story of a Friendship and the Quarrel that Ended It*" (Chicago: University of Chicago Press, 2004), 128.

revolution via a Soviet invasion in the same year, brought an end to Sartre's period of direct collaboration with the Stalinists.

Sartre's support for national liberation struggles in Algeria, Vietnam, Cuba and so on was based on the fundamental philosophical outlook of existentialism. Inherent to this outlook was the view that if the freedom of others is limited, then the freedom of all will be limited. It was in this context that he wrote one of his most hard-hitting political pieces, the preface to Franz Fanon's 1961 book "*The Wretched of the Earth*". There he took aim directly at the more respectable pacifist tendencies—the kind of people who call for an end to violence on both sides.

> "*If violence began this very evening, and if exploitation and oppression had never existed on the earth, perhaps the slogans of non-violence might end the quarrel*" *but if the whole regime, even your non-violent ideas, are conditioned by a thousand-year-old oppression, your passivity serves only to place you in the ranks of the oppressors*."

The significance of Sartre's stance in support of the Algerian independence can be understood only when viewed in the light of the intensely polarised atmosphere in France in those years. In October 1961, a demonstration of 30,000 Algerians in Paris was savagely attacked by police. More than 200 were killed, many drowning after being thrown into the Seine. At the same time, there was a wave of terrorist bombings by far-right French nationalists. As France's one of the most prominent intellectual, Sartre's stance put him at the centre of all this. His apartment was bombed on two occasions, and right-wing protesters marched down the street chanting "*shoot Sartre*". [75]

---

[75] The one shameful exception to Sartre's anti-colonial stance was his support for the establishment of Israel. He later came to be more sensitive to the Palestinian struggle, but in 1976, when he was awarded an honorary degree from the University of Jerusalem, he declared: "*I am as much pro-Palestinian as I am pro-Israeli and vice versa*".

Sartre's role in the struggle against the Algerian war, and his subsequent involvement in the early days of the anti-Vietnam war movement, cemented his reputation, particularly among the generation of young people. His radical reputation was further reinforced by his rejection, in 1964, of the Nobel Prize for Literature—which he refused on the ground that it was a part of an attempt to institutionalise him which he was opposed to for, according to him, "*The writer must refuse to allow himself to be turned into an Institution*".

In 1968, Sartre played an active role in the struggle, giving lectures to students at the occupied Sorbonne in Paris, and associating himself with the most militant elements. In a radio interview at the height of the protests, he railed against the idea of a "*reform*" of the university system, saying "*the only relationship that* [the students] *can have with this university is to smash it and in order to smash it there is only one solution: to take to the streets*". During this period, he was also strongly associated with the Maoist currents that were rapidly growing. In 1970, one of the main Maoist groups, *Gauche prolétarienne* (Proletarian Left), asked Sartre if he would agree to be listed as the editor of its paper because the two previous editors had been arrested and imprisoned. Sartre agreed, and even went so far as to sell the papers on the streets. He was arrested, but the government didn't dare send someone of Sartre's repute to jail. From the mid-70s until his death in April 1980, he drifted from active involvement in French political life.

"Sartre was not a Marxist"

"Sartre fails the test for membership in the Marxist family"

-- Raymond Aron

Marxism has seen a revival in recent years with preeminent works such as Slavoj Žižek's *The Relevance of the Communist Manifesto* (2019), Terry Eagleton's *Why Marx Was Right* (2011), and Alain Badiou's *The Communist Hypothesis* (2009/2010). In fall 2018, Ron Aronson published a remarkable essay with the title: "*The Philosophy of Our Time*,"1 in which he praises Sartre's existential Marxism as a possible "*philosophical foundation for today's revitalized critiques of capitalism.*" Aronson writes about Sartre's turn from his early individualism with his emphasis on absurdity, freedom, and responsibility to Marxism—of course, not a Stalinist version of Marxism, but a rather special version—existential Marxism.

In a recent article titled "*Sartre was not a Marxist*" [76], published shortly after Aronson's 2018 essay, Alfred Betschart (2019), however, argues that terms such as existential or existentialist Marxism or Marxist existentialism are cases of a *contradictio in adiecto*. Betschart points out that in its March 1966 issue, the French Communist journal *La Nouvelle Critique* asked the question: *Sartre est-il marxiste*? Is Sartre a Marxist? [77] At that time, the journal *La Nouvelle Critique*, originally founded by Sartre's pupil Jean Kanapa in 1948 and kept on an orthodox, i.e., Stalinist path until 1958, had taken a theoretical turn as it sought out new prospects for Marxism. The journal's answer to the question was a clear "*No.*" Sartre was deemed an antiquated humanist, operating with Hegelian rather than Marxist concepts, [78] a

[76] Betschart, Alfred: "*Sartre was not a Marxist*", Sartre Studies International Volume 25, Issue 2, 2019, pp. 77–91.

[77] André Gisselbrecht, Jean Roy, Jeanette Colombel, François Hincker, & Christine Glucksmann, "*Sartre est-il marxiste*?" La Nouvelle Critique. Revue du marxisme militant, March 1966.

[78] With Sartre, the relationship between lord and bondsman is more important than the dichotomy between bourgeoisie and proletariat. Unlike the Marxist concept of the one-way exploitation of the worker by the capitalist, the relationship between lord and bondsman is a mutual one. The lord, whether a colonialist, a manager, or a male human being, is not only an oppressor, but also an oppressed one

philosopher closer to Wilhelm Dilthey and Max Weber than Karl Marx.4 In 1962,

Betschart also draws our attention to Poland's leading Marxist philosopher of the early 1960s and far from an orthodox dogmatist Adam Schaff's book published in 1962 entitled: "*A Philosophy of Man, Marxism and Existentialism*". Though he readily conceded that existentialism had raised pertinent questions, Schaff insisted that there could be no marriage between existentialism and Marxism, such as the one proposed by Sartre in his "*Search for a Method*". According to Schaff, reconciling Marxist materialism and Sartrean idealism was as impossible as combining fire and water. [79] Danilo Pejović, a Croatian philosopher, a nonorthodox Marxist, and one of the founders of the journal '*Praxis*', had penned a positive review of Sartre in its first international issue in 1965. Although he did not discount the possibility that Sartre's thought might develop along the lines of the young György Lukács, Ernst Bloch, Theodor W. Adorno, or Herbert Marcuse, he described Sartre's existentialism as a typically French variation of radical nihilism. [80]

And it was not only philosophers with origins in orthodox Marxism who rejected the marriage of Marxism and existentialism. As Thomas Flynn noted in "*Sartre and Marxist Existentialism*", two other well-known experts in Marxism and existentialism, Maurice Merleau-Ponty in "*Adventures of the Dialectic*" and Sartre's old classmate and intellectual opponent Raymond Aron in "*Marxism*

[See, Sartre "Preface" in Frantz Fanon, "*The Wretched of the Earth*", in its corrected translation of 2004, trans. Richard Philcox, New York: Grove Press 2004, already in "*What is Literature? 1948*", Sartre had written that the bourgeois is tyrant and victim at the same time, Paris: Gallimard, 2013].

[79] Schaff, Adam, "*Marx oder Sartre*?", VEB Deutscher Verlag der Wissenschaften: Berlin 1965, p. 47.

[80] Pejovi, Danilo, "*Jean-Paul Sartre*," Praxis: Revue philosophique, 1, 1 Zagreb, 1965, p. 85.

and the Existentialists" were also clear that "*Sartre fails the test for membership in the Marxist family*". [81]

Betschart in his article also observes that the association of Sartre and Marxism was—and is still—one of the principal disparaging clichés deployed by the many "*Sartrophobes*" for whom Sartre the Marxist, Sartre the Commie, even Sartre the Maoist was an effective way of short-circuiting any discussion of Sartre's ideas. Alongside these detractors however, there are also a number of Sartre enthusiasts who persist in reading Sartre as an existentialist Marxist. Ron Aronson is one of the most prominent, but he does not stand alone. Mark Poster with "*Existential Marxism in Post-war France*" in 1975, John Lawler with "*The Existentialist Marxism*" in 1976, Thomas Flynn with "*Sartre and Marxist Existentialism*" in 1984, and more recently, Elizabeth Butterfield with "*Sartre and Posthumanist Humanism*" in 2012 have all made important contributions to the notion of an existential Marxism. [82] The most important argument in favour of existentialist Marxism can be found in Sartre himself, in his "*Search for a Method*", where he called Marxism the philosophy of our time—and even the philosophy beyond which we cannot go—while labelling existentialism an "ideology." However, Sartre himself referred to Marxist theory only rarely in his works after the "*Critique of Dialectical Reason*" (1960). The Critique itself consists mainly of points that contest Marxism, although the points put forward by Sartre are generally responses to questions raised by Marxist theory and practice. According to Betschart, the Critique must be considered rather as an anti-Marxist opus than as a great Marxist

---

[81] Flynn, Thomas, "*Sartre and Marxist Existentialism*", Chicago: University of Chicago Press 1984, p. 176.

[82] Mark Poster: "*Existential Marxism in Post-war France: From Sartre to Althusse*", Princeton University Press, 1975. James Lawler: "*The Existentialist Marxism of Jean-Paul Sartre*" Amsterdam: B. R. Grüner, 1976. Flynn, "*Sartre and Marxist Existentialism*", Chicago: University of Chicago Press 1984, Elizabeth Butterfield, "*Sartre and Posthumanist Humanism*", Frankfurt: Peter Lang, 2012.

treatise as Aronson claims. Whereas in Marxist theory, classes are the prime agents of history, they are reduced to what Sartre calls "*series*" in the Critique. Classes do not act in Sartre's eyes; at best they form milieus. In this way, Sartre implicitly contests the Marxist idea of a revolution by the proletariat. [83]

In this end, it is pertinent to note that Sartre, with both his philosophy and life, is synonymous with controversy. It is, therefore, only natural there will be views, both for and against, on any important aspect of his life. On the question, therefore, whether he was a Marxist or not, it is only fair to let Sartre have the final word:

> "[Q]. *You have defined the Critique de la raison dialectique as a work opposed to the Communists and yet endeavoring to be Marxist.*

---

83 "It is Sartre's term of the "group-infusion" that comes closest to the Marxist understanding of a class driven revolution. It is this concept, developed in relation to the storming of the Bastille in Paris in 1789 and possibly the first Russian revolution in 1905, that anchors Sartre's concise theory about the development of groups. They are the real actors in history. Groups first start with voluntary congregations of people, like those playing soccer in a park on a Sunday afternoon. At the next stage of its evolution, the pledged group appears. This group is not yet well organized, but power and authority are already discernible attributes in the pledged group. The early Communist groups, e.g. the First International (1864–1876) and the Russian Social Democratic Labour Party (RSDLP) before the February Revolution, were such pledged groups. These groups have however a congenital defect: what Sartre called "terror-fraternity." The splits between Marxists and anarchists in the First International and between Mensheviks and Bolsheviks in the RSDLP were the forerunners of Stalin's terror regime from the 1930s to his death in 1953. For Sartre, the prerequisite of a successful revolution is the existence of a pledged or organized group. Sartre's insistence, in his discussion in 1953 with Claude Lefort, Merleau-Ponty's friend and former pupil, that a successful revolution can only be made by a party, i.e. a pledged or organized group, and not by a class as such, is a strong critique of the Marxist concept of revolution: it is never the proletariat class that creates a revolution, but always a group. After the discussion with Lefort, Merleau-Ponty called Sartre an "Ultra-Bolshevik" in Adventures of the Dialectic— and he was not wrong. In short, one might say that Sartre even goes a step further than Vladimir Lenin, the most important Bolshevik theoretician, by leaving out the fig leaf of the proletariat in whose name the Communist party claimed its revolution." [See: Betschart, Alfred: "Sartre was not a Marxist", Sartre Studies International Volume 25, Issue 2, 2019, p.70.

Sartre: Opposed to the Communists, certainly. But Marxist is a word that I used a bit lightly then. At that time, I considered the Critique to be Marxist: I was convinced of it. But I have changed my mind since then. Today, I think that, in certain areas, the Critique is close to Marxism, but it is not a Marxist work. [...]

[Q]: *I myself was bothered by your distinction. I saw the existentialism of the Critique as an attempt at synthesizing Marxism and going beyond it, whereas you said that existentialism was only an enclave of Marxism.*

Sartre: Yes, but that was my mistake. It cannot be an enclave, because of my idea of freedom, and therefore, it is ultimately a separate philosophy. I do not at all think that ultimately this philosophy is Marxist. It cannot ignore Marxism; it is linked to it, just as some philosophies are linked to others without, however, being contained by them. But now I do not consider it at all a Marxist philosophy." [84]

----

[84] Sartre and Rybalka, "*The Interview*," p.20.

Chapter 14

Clash of the Titans

"The Sartres 'justify Evil by justifying the justification of it.'"

--- Raymond Aron

Aron attacks Sartre

Raymond Aron, French philosopher, sociologist and journalist, was a redoubtable member of the French intellectual elite. A classmate of Sartre and topper of his batch at the École, Aron's philosophical prowess was such that he could easily match his longtime friend.

Raymond Aron

Aron was opposed to Marxism. It is ironic for he was a thorough reader of Marx. In fact, he was better read in Marx than most French Marxists. Therefore, although at times despised, he could never be marginalized or disregarded.

Aron was critical of Marxism as he saw it as reneging on some of the basic advances made by human civilisations, such as the freedom of enquiry, freedom of controversy, and the freedom of criticism.

In a damning criticism of the widespread intellectual adherence in his time to Marxism –it was almost fashionable to do so - Aron wrote his influential book titled "*L' Opium des intellectuels*" ("*The Opium of the Intellectuals*"). The book was published in 1955. [85]

A major focus of Aron's criticism in his book was aimed at Sartre & his idea to fuse Marxist thought with existentialist thinking. This, in his opinion, relegated prudence from politics.

Aron and Sartre were on opposite sides of the Cold War divide. Aron was against violent extremism of communism. Sartre's inclination was to the leftist; he believed in revolutionary violence for justice and freedom

Aron was of the view that there was a form of intellectual dishonesty or hypocrisy at work in his time period, where some people were extremely critical of certain forms of government or society (such as, *capitalist democracy*), but indifferent towards crimes and violations committed in societies claiming to manifest the 'correct' ideology (*Stalin's regime in Russia*). This seemed to him a kind of intellectual dogmatism and fanaticism regardless of empirical evidence against it. For Aron, such disregard of the French intelligentsia, including Sartre, for the real implications of

---

[85] Aron, Raymond: *"The Opium of the Intellectuals"*, Transaction Publishers, New Brunswick (USA) and London (UK), 2011.

their theoretical pronouncements signified the height of irresponsibility.

Though he was a close friend of both Sartre and de Beauvoir, Aron was so angry with the way they justified Stalin's brutalities that he published a letter declaring end of their friendship.

Solzhenitsyn rebuffs Sartre: Aron joins the fray

Solzhenitsyn, the famous Russian writer, and Nobel Laureate, had an aversion for Sartre. It was so intense that he refused to meet Sartre when he and de Beauvoir visited Russia in 1963, in the post-Stalin era, as guests of honour of the Soviet Writers' Union.

In his book "*The Oak and the Calf*", Solzhenitsyn disparagingly calls Sartre the *"ruler of minds"* in the West. He also wonders *"whether Sartre discerned in my refusal the depth of our aversion to him."*

Aleksandr Solzhenitsyn

Raymond Aron and Aleksandr Solzhenitsyn, both were opposed to Communist totalitarianism, Aron was an ardent admirer of the Russian writer. For him, Solzhenitsyn was more than a political figure; he represented an unconditional "spiritual" commitment to truth and liberty.

In 1976, Aron published a powerful reflection on the encounter between Solzhenitsyn and Sartre. Written for a "*festschrift*" [86] for his friend Manès Sperber, the Austrian-born novelist and essayist, this piece is Aron's most insightful tribute to Solzhenitsyn and arguably his most scathing critique of Sartre.

Recalling that Solzhenitsyn had refused to meet Sartre in 1963 when he visited Russia, Aron was of the view Solzhenitsyn's refusal to meet Sartre was not at all a matter of surprise; he wrote:

> "*As a personality Sartre embodies everything which Solzhenitsyn loathes: the rejection of moral guidelines, the refusal to accept the age-old distinction between good and evil, the sacrifice of men's lives and the justification of crimes by appeals to an indefinite future ('indefinite' in all its senses), in short, the evil of ideology...*" For Sartre, "*Marxism is the unsurpassable philosophy of our era," a dogmatic and even "stupid. ... Sartre defended the Soviet Union during the darkest days of Stalinism before heading off to Cuba to befriend Castro in the early years of the Cuban revolution. His heart and head always leaped to the Left.*" [87]

In Aron's pungent formulation, the Sartres *"justify Evil by justifying the justification of it."*

Aron believed if they had ended up meeting, the dialogue between Solzhenitsyn and Sartre would have amounted to nothing.

----

[86] A collection of writings by different authors presented as a tribute or memorial in honour of a scholar.

[87] Aron, Raymond: *"Solzhenitsyn and European Leftism"*, **published in** *Survey* 100/101, Summer/Autumn, 1976.

Chapter 15
Sartre: Was he Stalin's stooge?

"[A] ***devil's advocate to be despised more than the devil, because the advocate was smarter"***

--- Clive James on Sartre

A major charge against Sartre is that he acted as Stalin's stooge and blindly supported the atrocities committed during Stalin's totalitarian regime.

In a scathing attack on Sartre, the well- known Australian author, critic, and, poet Clive James, in his book *"Cultural Amnesia: Necessary Memories from History and the Arts"* (2007) [88], called him *"a devil's advocate to be despised more than the devil, because the advocate was smarter."* He sarcastically remarked, though Sartre never actually killed anybody, *"he excused many who did, and most of those never actually killed anybody, either: They just gave orders for their subordinates to do so.* "He criticised Sartre's philosophy as being *"all a pose"*.

---

[88] James, Clive: *"Jean-Paul Sartre"* in *"Cultural Amnesia: Necessary Memories from History and the Arts"*, W.W. Norton & Company, March, 2007.

Clive James

An apologist for tyranny and terror: Brian C. Anderson

The American writer and Editor of City Journal published by the Manhattan Institute for Policy Research, Brian C. Anderson, in his article *"The Absolute Intellectual",* branded Sartre as an apologist for tyranny and terror and a blind supporter of Stalinism, Maoism and Castro's regime in Cuba. [89]

[89] Anderson, Brian C.: *"The Absolute Intellectual"* Hoover Institution, Policy Review, February 1, 2004.

Brian C. Anderson

Hypocrite*: *Michael Walzer

In his preface to the book "*The Wretched of the Earth" (*Frantz Fanon, Grove Press, 1961), Sartre wrote:

> *"To shoot down a European is to kill two birds with one stone, to destroy an oppressor and the man he oppresses at the same time: there remains a dead man and a free man,"*

Sartre's comment drew considerable flak for it justified the killing of European civilians by the National Liberation Front of Algeria during the Algerian War. Michael Walzer, the noted American political theorist and professor emeritus at the Institute for Advanced Study in Princeton, New Jersey, called Sartre a hypocrite saying if Sartre sincerely believed in what he had advocated, then, as a European, he should have volunteered to be killed.

Michael Walzer

Overhyped: Robert Fulford

Some critics strongly feel that Sartre has been overhyped. He cleverly built an image larger than himself. In an article titled *"The last words of a toxic intellectual"* published in "*The National Post"* *(22 September 2007*), the Canadian journalist, editor, and essayist Robert Fulford sarcastically remarked:

> *"Once the public freely accepts that someone is "great," that conviction becomes impossible to dislodge. Jean-Paul Sartre, philosopher, novelist, playwright and self-promoter, proved this axiom....He was always a favourite writer of people who didn't read him but liked to read about him."*[90]

---

[90] Fulford, Robert: *"The last words of a toxic intellectual"*, The National Post, 22 September, 2007.

Robert Fulford

Overrated: Vladimir Nabokov

Vladimir Nabokov, the famous Russian novelist, poet and author of "*Lolita*", was also of the opinion that Sartre was overrated.

Vladimir Nabokov

In March 1949, Nabokov wrote a devastatingly dismissive review, for the New York Times Book Review, of the Sartre's first novel "*La Nausee*" (English translation by Lloyd Alexander):

> *"Sartre's name, I understand, is associated with a fashionable brand of cafe philosophy and since for every so-called "existentialist" one finds quite a few "suctorialists" (if I may coin a polite term), this made-in- England translation of Sartre's first novel, "La Nausee" ... should enjoy some success."*

Nabokov, in fact, thrusts even deeper and observes:

> *"Whether from the viewpoint of literature, La Nausee was worth translating at all is another question. It belongs to that tense-looking but really very loose type of writing, which has been popularized by many second-raters – Barbusse, Celine, and so forth. Somewhere behind looms Dostoevsky at his worst, and still farther is Old Eugene Sue, to whom the melodramatic Russian owed so much.*
>
> *.... When an author inflicts his idle and arbitrary fancy on a helpless person whom he has invented for that purpose, a lot of talent is need to have the trick work. One has no special quarrel with Roquentin when he decides that the world exists. But the task to make the world exist as a world of art was beyond Sartre's powers."*

When Nabokov was asked by the Times to review Sartre's *"What is literature"*, Nabokov flatly declined saying "*I have read the French original and consider it trash. Frankly, I do not think it is worth reviewing.*" [91]

---

[91] Boyd, Brian: *"Vladimir Nabokov: The American Years"*, Princeton University Press, Princeton, New Jersey, 1991, p. 138

In 1948, the Roman Catholic Church included Sartre's works in the "List of Prohibited Books".

Sartre targeted by Communists: Ettu, Brute?

"If jackals could learn to operate a typewriter and hyenas to push a fountain pen", they would produce no doubt something strongly resembling the writings of the Henry Millers, the Eliots, the Malraux and sundry Sartres.

--- Alexander Fadeyev

Ironically, Sartre was also a target of attack by Communists. He was among the writers about whom Alexander Fadeyev, Soviet novelist, and Chairman of the Soviet Writers' Union, made disparaging remarks at the World Congress of Intellectuals held at Wroclaw, Poland in August, 1948.

Alexander Fadeyev

In his address at the World Congress, Fadeyev excoriated well-regarded literary personalities like Eugene O'Neill and John Dos Passos, calling them *"literary agents of reaction"*. Continuing in the same tenor, he said *"If jackals could learn to operate a typewriter and hyenas to push a fountain pen"*, they would produce no doubt something strongly resembling the writings of the Henry Millers, the Eliots, the Malraux and sundry Sartres.[92]

Ironically, therefore, despite his well-known leaning to the Soviet Bloc, particularly during the period prior to 1956, Sartre was not spared by the left.

Later as he became increasingly disillusioned with Stalin's regime, Sartre wrote *"the politics of Stalinist Communism are incompatible with the honest exercise of the literary profession."* He also argued that Stalinism had rendered Marxism sterile, because you cannot turn *"dialectics into formulae for catechism."*

In Defence of Sartre

Unfair to call him Devil's Advocate: David Detmer

In his book titled "*Sartre Explained: From Bad Faith to Authenticity*" (2009)), David Detmer, Professor of Philosophy, Purdue University Northwest and the author of "*Freedom as a Value*", admits while for a major part of his life, Sartre was independent, non-Stalinist, leftist, he took many indefensible stand in support of authoritarian Eastern Bloc regimes, especially during the 1952-56 period. However, Detmer argues, there are at least three points that should be considered for proper appreciation of Sartre's stance.

---

[92] Feinberg, Melissa: "*Curtain of Lies: The Battle over Truth in Stalinist Eastern Europe*", Oxford University Press, 2017.

David Detmer

Firstly, according to Detmer, Sartre's support for Stalin during the period in question was grudging and not spontaneous. This is apparent from his comment in 1951: *"To the extent I am inspired by a rather broad Marxism, I am an enemy for Stalinist communists."* In spite of this, Sartre supported Stalin and the USSR because the Cold War did not leave for him any space for neutrality or independence. He probably thought oppression in the communist bloc would eventually be over when Cold War tensions would diminish.

Secondly, Sartre's journal, Detmer points out, was the first to expose and condemn the existence of "*Gulag*", Soviet labour camps, devoting an entire issue to this one topic in 1950. Sartre himself had said *"there is no Socialism when one in twenty citizens is in a camp."* It is, therefore, not fair to say Sartre blindly supported the atrocities committed by Stalinist regime. On the contrary, he was rather vigilant and chastised them whenever the occasion so warranted.

Finally, from 1956 till the end of his life, Sartre always condemned misdeeds committed by socialist or communist countries. He condemned the Soviet attack on Hungary in 1956 and said: *"I condemn the Russian aggression completely and unreservedly."* When the French Communist Party defended the Soviet invasion, he declared: *"it is not possible, and never will be possible to renew relations with the men who are in charge of the PCF at the moment"*, and he really severed his relations with the French communists. He condemned the Soviet invasion of Czechoslovakia, calling the Soviets *"war criminals"*. In 1972, he criticised the political oppression in Cuba, although he was an enthusiastic supporter of the Castro revolution in its earlier years.

Sartre supported Israel when it was denounced by Soviet propaganda after the 1967 war and in the 70's, he expressed contempt and hatred for the Russian and French Communist Parties.

With a track record like this, would it be fair to call him Devil's Advocate? [93]

"The conscience of the world": Herbert Marcuse

Herbert Marcuse, the well-known German-American philosopher, sociologist, and a prominent member of the Frankfurt School of critical social analysis, called him *"the conscience of the world."*

---

[93] Detmer, David: *"Sartre Explained: From Bad Faith to Authenticity"*, Open Court Publishing Company, Chicago and La Salle, Illinois, p. 13, 2009.

Herbert Marcuse

Who wins, who loses?

Now, with his report card laid bare, it is for us to assess if Sartre was really "Stalin's stooge", "*a devil's advocate*" and a "blind supporter of leftism" as alleged – or, was he a living embodiment of his own philosophy of "Existentialism" that he so passionately preached. Being "*condemned to freedom*", was it not his candid response to his own "*anguish of freedom*"?

It is for each one of us to find one's own answer. But one thing is for sure; even if Sartre is taken to the gallows for being a "*bad man*" or a "*Devil's Advocate*" as he has sometimes been labelled, he must not be spared the credit of having lived his entire life "*authentically*", and not in "*bad faith*" that he so intensely despised.

Chapter 16

Jean-Paul Sartre & Albert Camus: A Tale of Two friends

"[The] ***new literature in France,*** **[is]** ***"result of the resistance movement and the war,*** **[and]** ***its best representative is 30-year-old Albert Camus."***

--- Jean-Paul Sartre

A Tale of Two Friends

They were from different background. Unlike Sartre who was from the upper reaches of French society, Albert Camus, the noted French-Algerian philosopher, and author, was born into poverty. They met in Paris during the 'Occupation' and grew closer after the Second World War.

Jean-Paul Sartre and Albert Camus first met in June 1943, at the opening of Sartre's play "*The Flies*". Sartre was standing in the lobby, when, Simone de Beauvoir writes, *"a dark-skinned young man came up and introduced himself: it was Albert Camus."* His novel "*The Stranger*", published a year earlier, was a literary sensation, and his philosophical essay "*The Myth of Sisyphus*" had appeared six months back. The young man from Algiers was marooned in France by the war. He was convalescing from an exacerbation of his chronic tuberculosis in *Le Panelier*, near Chambon. He was married, but his wife had stayed behind in North Africa. He wanted to meet Sartre—whose fiction he had reviewed years earlier and who had just published a long article on Camus's own books. It was a brief encounter. *"I'm Camus,"* he said. Sartre immediately *"found him a most likeable personality."*

In November, Camus moved to Paris to start working as a reader for his (and Sartre's) publisher, Gallimard, and their friendship began in earnest. At their first get-together at the *Café de Flore*—where Sartre, de Beauvoir and their other existentialist associates kept themselves warm, ate, and socialized—the three started off once again, Camus and Sartre sharing their regard for the French surrealist essayist and poet Francis Ponge's Le Parti pris des choses. What "*led to the ice being broken*" between them, according to de Beauvoir, was Camus's passion for the theatre. Camus had led an amateur political theatre troupe in Algiers. Sartre talked to Camus of his new play *"No Exit"* and *"suggested that Camus should play the lead and stage it. Camus hesitated at first, but when Sartre pressed the point he agreed. ...The readiness with which Camus flung himself into this venture endeared him to us."*

Sartre was pleased with Camus's work in the role of Garcin, but his financial backer withdrew; *"this man's wife, who was to be showcased in "No Exit", was arrested for suspected Resistance activity."* Sartre was then offered the chance to present the play in a professional production on the Paris stage, and Camus obligingly backed out. But the friendship was cemented. *"His youth and independence created bonds between us: we were all solitaries, who had developed without the aid of any 'school'; we belonged to no group or clique."*

They were icons of the era. Newspapers reported on their daily movements: Sartre holed up at Les Deux Magots, Camus the peripatetic of Paris. After the war, as the world was trying to adapt to new realities, Sartre and Camus gave voice to the mood of the day. [94] Europe had been immolated, but the ashes left by war created the space to imagine a new world. The people, particularly the young generation, looked to Sartre and Camus to articulate what that new world might look like. 'We were,' remembered the fellow philosopher Simone de Beauvoir, 'to provide the post-war era with its ideology.' They wrote about "existentialism', they wrote about the "absurdity" of the world – a world without purpose and without value. People, they said, are '*free*' --- burdened only to live and act '*authentically*'.

There were many commonalities between the two friends. They were both storytellers, playwrights and essayists, literature and theatre critics, philosophers and editors in chief. They had the same publisher.

And there was yet another commonality. Both preferred the company of women to that of men. "*Why women*?" Camus wondered in his diary in 1951. His answer: "*I cannot stand the company of men. They flatter or they judge. I can stand neither of the two.*" Back in 1940, Sartre used nearly the same logic in his diary noting that he "*gets horribly bored in the company of men*".

There have been speculations of underlying rivalry and jealousy between the two friends. No one would know the truth; but the tone was always friendly- at least till they fell out over ideological issues. When Sartre travelled to the United States in 1945 and spoke about "*new literature in France*," he presented it as the "*result of the resistance movement and the war,*" adding that "*its best representative is 30-year-old Albert Camus.*

---

94 Camus was an ardent lover of nature. He loved Algiers intensely, in particular the white sands of its beaches and the blue waters of the Mediterranean. This sensibility of his to natural beauty may have helped him in his search for a Supreme Being. With his passionate belief in justice for all, he felt outraged at the blood being shed in his native Algeria during the revolt of 1955.

Both Sartre and Camus were awarded the Nobel Prize for literature – after they had fallen out in 1952 summer. Camus accepted his award in 1957. Sartre declined it when awarded to him seven years later.

Chapter 17

Sartre & Camus: Friends no more

From the political perspective, both Sartre and Camus were of the view the most unjustly treated group was the workers'- the proletariat, shackled as they are to their labour and shorn of their humanity. For their liberation to a world with freedom and justice, a new political order is a must.

But as time rolled on, reports of violation of rights of freedom of expression, horrors of labour camps and violence under the Communist USSR regime sent Camus on a different trajectory. Finally, in October 1951, Camus published a philosophical essay *"L'Homme Révolté" ("The Rebel").* In it, he advocated for a peaceful socialism that would not resort to revolutionary violence.

Albert Camus

Jean-Paul Sartre

> *"Absolute freedom is the right of the strongest to dominate; it mocks at justice.'* Camus wrote, while *"absolute justice is achieved by the suppression of all contradictions; therefore, it denies freedom. To be fruitful, the two ideas must find their limits in each other."*

The conflict between justice and freedom, Camus stressed, requires constant re-balancing, political moderation; for acceptance and celebration of our most cherished object - our humanity.

> *"I choose freedom." he said, "For even if justice is not realised, freedom maintains the power of protest against injustice and keeps communication open."*

Sartre read The "Rebel" with disgust. As far as he was concerned, it was possible to achieve both, perfect justice and freedom, through communism for which revolutionary violence would be in order.

The split between the two friends was a media sensation. *"Les Temps Modernes",* the journal edited by Sartre, published a nasty review of *"The Rebel".* What was more outrageous, Sartre commissioned Francis Jeanson, a junior editor in his office to write a hatchet job of "*Rebel*".

Camus was upset by the review – which took twenty pages to say that he was basically too stupid to understand Hegel or Marx and his opinion was, therefore, worthless; but just as upset that Sartre gave it to a young unknown, suggesting that his work was not even worthy of his attention.

On June 30, 1952 Camus sent a seventeen-page letter to the journal *Les Temps Modernes*, a response to Francis Jeanson's harshly critical review of his book, '*The Rebel*'. The letter was not addressed to Jeanson, but to "*M. Le Directeur,*" i.e., Sartre. Its penultimate paragraph was direct and personal:

> "*I am beginning to get a little tired of seeing myself—and even more, of seeing former militants who have never refused the struggles of their time—endlessly receive lessons in efficacy from critics who have never done anything more than turn their theater seat in the direction of history.*"

At this point Sartre himself took up the cudgel and wrote in an open editorial:

> "*My dear Camus,*
>
> "*Our friendship was not an easy one, but I shall miss it*"; he accused Camus of "*philosophical incompetence*" labelling his "*reasoning inaccurate and* [his] *thoughts vague and banal*". He concluded his editorial saying,
>
> "*Unfortunately, you attacked me so deliberately and in such an unpleasant tone that I cannot remain silent without losing face. I shall, therefore, reply: without anger, but, for the first time since I've known you, without mincing my words. A mix of melancholy, conceit and vulnerability on your part has always deterred people from telling you unvarnished truths.* [...] *Sooner or later, someone would have told you this, so it might as well be me.*"

Sartre's response ended the friendship; he also destroyed nearly all their correspondences. The two men never spoke to each other again.

The rift, in the summer of 1952, divided them. The two former friends never spoke again; although they continued to publicly disagree until Camus's death. [95][96] Sartre continued on a Marxist political platform; Camus confronted the absurd.

----

[95] It was at the *Café de la Mairie* at the Place Saint Sulpice where Sartre and Camus met for the last time in 1951, having worked together for years in the radical left wing newspaper Combat. They never met again.

[96] Recently, in 2014, a previously unknown letter sent by Camus to Sartre has surfaced that shows the two men had been dearest friends only months before they fell out. The undated letter, authenticated by experts, is believed to have been written in the spring of 1951. "[It] *was acquired by an autograph collector in the 1970s and kept in a frame above his fireplace ever since*," said Nicolas Lieng of the Le Pas Sage Bookstore, which specialises in 19th and 20th-century literature. "*It was sold to a private French collector, who owns one of the most beautiful Camus collections, a week ago*," he added.

Opening "*my dear Sartre*", the long letter signed by Camus, ends with "*I shake your hand.*" In the letter, Camus recommends that Sartre considers an actress named Aminda Valls for his new play. Camus described the actress, who was also a friend of the French stage star Maria Casarès, as a "*Spanish republican*" and "*marvel of humanity*".

At that time, Sartre was preparing to stage his play *Le diable et le bon dieu*, that was premiered in 1951 in Paris's Théâtre Antoine. While Casarès got the role of Hilda, Valls did not end up taking part in the production.

[Source: Kunova, Marcel: "*Albert Camus and Jean-Paul Sartre: 'Lost' letter shows philosophers were dearest friends before their bitter falling-out*", Independent, 26 November 2014.]

Chapter 18

Sartre and Camus: At daggers drawn

What, specifically, was so wrong with "The Rebel"?

But what, specifically, was so wrong with '*The Rebel*'? The book purports to analyse the tragic consequences of rebellion turning to revolution. With the "*death of God*," the history of which Camus analyses in detail, the universal values that might have served to restrain historical rebellion disappeared. Thus followed the excesses of the French Revolution, the "*irrational terror*" of fascism, and the "*rational terror*" of Marxism. And for the last one, its "*scientific*" certainty that a peaceful, harmonious, glorious future lay in store for humankind entails that no moral scruples need to stand in the way of hastening the arrival of that new dawn—hence Stalinism.

Camus argues in his book for a sense of moderation, rooted not in God but in human nature, a sense of those transcendent values that shine forth in the act of rebellion, values that tend to disappear when rebellion becomes revolution.

Sartre, it is said, initially asked his people at *Les Temps Modernes* that, for the sake of his friendship with Camus, nothing bad be said in the critique of the book, but no one from the journal stepped forward to do the review? Simone de Beauvoir recalls, "*none of us could think of anything good*" to say. Ultimately, Sartre dropped the restrictive condition, and gave the assignment to the young unknown Jeanson.

But why so? Camus, after all, was not a reactionary. In *The Rebel*, he explicitly endorses "*revolutionary trade unionism*;" he calls for the "*immediate suppression of the death penalty*"; he sees "*Scandinavian societies today*" as approximately just, and hence worthy of emulation. Camus doesn't reject all violence, although he insists that it "*must be bound, if it cannot be avoided, to a personal responsibility.* [...] *Authentic acts of rebellion will only consent to take up arms for institutions that limit violence, not for those which codify it* [...] *and that it would allow absolute freedom of speech.*"

In his reply to Camus, Sartre's basic argument is that Camus has abandoned the struggle to change the world: "*When a man sees the present struggles merely as the imbecile duel between equally despicable monsters, I contend that that man has already left us: he has gone off alone to his corner and is sulking.*"

Sartre, in his reply, went on further to say that, in particular, what was missing both from *The Rebel* and from Camus's worldview was any real sense of class struggle. According to him, the root problem is Camus's conception of history:

> "*You remain within our great classical tradition, which, since Descartes and with the exception of Pascal, have been entirely hostile to history*"

Sartre acknowledges Camus' commitment for devoting himself "*unreservedly to the Resistance*" at a great cost, but is of the view that Camus' "*first contact with history assumed for ...* [him] *the aspect of sacrifice*"; he tells Camus,

> "*In short, it was not your intention to "make history," as Marx says, but to prevent it from being made. Proof lies in the fact that, after the war, you merely had in mind a return to the status quo ante.* [...] *After serving your five years with history, you thought you (and the whole of humanity) could return to the despair in which man must find his happiness.*"

"How we loved you in those days," Sartre laments. *"We too were neophytes of history and endured it with repugnance.* [But that's because we didn't understand…] *that the war of 1940 was but one mode of historicity--neither more nor less so than the years that preceded it."* But now, appraising the situation differently, Sartre accuses Camus (and perhaps his former self) of giving up on the real struggles of concrete persons in order to grapple with the metaphysical anguish occasioned by a world in which a supposedly good God lets innocent children die in agony. For Sartre, these anguished ruminations are—to people with *real* problems—*"mere aristocratic amusements."*

Sartre tells Camus that everything became clear to him after rereading "*Letter to a German Friend*" (published after the war), in which Camus says, "*for years now, you have tried to get me to enter History.*"

> ""*"Good Lord,"* *I* [Sartre] *said to myself, "since he believes he stands outside history, no wonder he lays down his conditions before coming inside." Like a girl testing the water with her toe and asking, "Is it warm?" you regard history warily. You stick in a finger, then very quickly pull it out again, asking, "Has it a meaning?" You didn't hesitate in 1941, but then you were being asked to make a sacrifice. It was quite simply a question of preventing the Hitlerian madness from smashing a world where solitary elation was still possible for some, and you were willing to pay the price for your future moments of elation."*

Continuing further, Sartre pointed out,

> "*Things are different today. It is no longer a question of defending the status quo, but of changing it.* […] *If I thought as you do, that history is a pool of mud and blood, I would do as you do,* […] *and look twice before diving in.* […] *But*

> *suppose you receive the answer Marx would give you: "History does nothing. [...] It is real living men who do everything; history is merely the activity of human beings pursuing their own ends." If this is true, the person who believes he is moving away from history will cease to share his contemporaries' ends, and will be sensible only to the absurdity of human restlessness. But if he rails against that restlessness, he will, against his will, re-enter the historical cycle, for he will involuntarily provide the side that is on the defensive (that is to say, the one whose culture is dying) with arguments for discouraging the other.*"

The philosophical battle between the two friends ended their friendship.

Talking of Camus, wrote Andy Martin at the "*New York Times philosophy blog*", he is "*more like Samuel Beckett; all alone, in the night, between continents, far away from everything.*" [97][98]

Eight years later, Camus died. [99]

They should have been a dream team. But it turned into a duel unto death.

----

97 Schweickart, David: "*Sartre, Camus and a Marxism for the 21st Century*", Loyola University Chicago, Sartre Studies International, 24, 2: 24, 2018. Retrieved from Loyola eCommons, Philosophy: Faculty Publications and Other Works.

98 Just after his quarrel with Sartre, Camus wrote a very positive preface to a book called "*Lenin's Moscow*", the memoir of Alfred Rosmer. Rosmer was a pioneer French Communist, later an opponent of Stalin, who had worked closely with Lenin and Trotsky in the early years of the Communist International.

99 Aronson, Ronald: "*Camus and Sartre: The Story of a Friendship and the Quarrel that Ended It*", University of Chicago Press, University of Chicago, 2004.

Chapter 19

Death of Albert Camus: Sartre pays Tribute

Camus was "probably my last good friend".

--- Jean-Paul Sartre

On January 4, 1960, Camus was killed in a car accident on a drive back to Paris, at the age of 46. Though the two never formally reconciled, Sartre penned a heartfelt tribute to his former friend in "*The Reporter Magazine" ("Tribute to Albert Camus")* - a tribute as warm as one would pay only to the most beloved. In deep appreciation of his friend and antagonist's solitude and stubborn resoluteness, Sartre wrote:

> *"He and I had quarrelled. A quarrel doesn't matter -- even if those who quarrel never see each other again -- just another way of living together without losing sight of one another in the narrow little world that is allotted us. It didn't keep me from thinking of him, from feeling that his eyes were on the book or newspaper I was reading and wondering: "What does he think of it? What does he think of it at this moment?"* ...

> *"He represented in our time the latest example of that long line of moralists whose works constitute perhaps the most original element in French letters. His obstinate humanism, narrow and pure, austere, and sensual, waged an uncertain war against the massive and formless events of the time. But on the other hand, through his dogged rejections he reaffirmed, at the heart of our epoch, against*

the Machiavellians and against the Idol of realism, the existence of the moral issue.

In a way, he was that resolute affirmation. Anyone who read or reflected encountered the human values he held in his fist; he questioned the political act. One had to avoid him or fight him-he was indispensable to that tension which makes intellectual life what it is. His very silence, these last few years, had something positive about it: This Descartes of the Absurd refused to leave the safe ground of morality and venture on the uncertain paths of practicality. We sensed this and we also sensed the conflicts he kept hidden, for ethics, taken alone, both requires and condemns revolt.

We were waiting; we had to wait; we had to know. Whatever he did or decided subsequently, Camus would never have ceased to be one of the chief forces of our cultural activity or to represent in his way the history of France and of this century...." [100]

The two friends had parted ways over their philosophical differences. But to Sartre, Camus was never an "*outsider*".

Fifteen years later, a 70-year-old Sartre, asked about his relationship to Camus in an interview for *Les Temps Modernes*, said: Camus was "*probably my last good friend".*

----

[100]Jean-Paul Sartre: "*Tribute to Albert Camus*" published in "Camus: A Collection of Critical Essays" (ed.) by Jacqueline Brian and Mary Danu sis Cooper, Germaine Bree, Englewood Cliffs, NJ: Prentice Hall, 1962.

Chapter 20

Sartre refuses Nobel Prize

"The writer must refuse to allow himself to be turned into an Institution"

--- Jean-Paul Sartre, on his refusal of the Nobel Prize for Literature awarded to him in 1964

In 1945, Sartre refused the *"Legion d'Honneur" ("Legion of Honour")*, the highest French order of merit for military and civil merits, established in 1802 by Napoleon Bonaparte.

In 1964, the 59-year-old Sartre was awarded Nobel Prize for Literature. But, to the utter shock of the entire world, he declined it. He was the first Nobel laureate to voluntarily decline the prize.

After the award was announced, Sartre was interviewed by journalists outside the Paris flat of Simone de Beauvoir and told the press he rejected the Nobel Prize for fear that it would limit the impact of his writing. He also expressed regrets that circumstances had given his decision "*the appearance of a scandal*". [101]

For some time after he was awarded the prize, Sartre tried to escape the media by hiding in the house of Simone's sister Helene in Goxwiller, Alsace.

---

101 "*Sartre and his Kafkaesque Nobel Prize moment, 1964*", Belle Meade Books, October 22, 2010.

Hélène de Beauvoir's house in Goxwiller, where Sartre tried to hide from the media after being awarded the Nobel Prize

Why he refused Nobel?: Sartre's rejoinder

"If I sign myself Jean-Paul Sartre, it is not the same thing as signing Jean-Paul Sartre, Nobel Laureate."

-- Jean-Paul Sartre

The Nobel Prize to Sartre was announced on 22 October 1964.Sartre had already made up his mind. He declined it.

The circumstances in which the Nobel prize was granted to him turned out to be somewhat Kafkaesque because of a bureaucratic slip-up on the part of the Nobel committee. A week before the award was to be announced, on reading in the October 15 "Figaro littéraire", in the Swedish correspondent's column, that the choice of the Swedish Academy was tending toward him, Sartre had sent a polite letter to the Nobel Institute expressing his wish to be removed from the list of nominees. He also declared he would not accept the award if it were presented to him. The letter was not read in time and Sartre was named the Nobel laureate in literature to the embarrassment of everyone involved; it was the first instance when the recipient of this prize voluntarily declined it. As the propriety of such refusal began to be widely debated, some explanation on the part of Sartre appeared to be necessary. [102]

In *Le Figaro* (23 October, 1964) and later in "*Les Lettresfrancaises*" (29 October and 4 November 1964) under the title *"L'ecrivain doit refuser de se laisser transformer en institution"* (*"The writer must refuse to allow himself to be turned into an Institution"*), Sartre clarified his position.

At the outset, he expressed regret for the fuss caused by his refusal to accept the Prize; but he was quick to add: *"I didn't know that the Nobel Prize was awarded without the recipient being asked for his opinion and I thought there was time to block it."*

Elaborating further, Sartre said he did not wish to be "*transformed*" by such an award, and did not want to take sides in an East vs. West cultural struggle by accepting the award. His decision, he said, had no relation with the Swedish Academy or the Nobel Prize in itself. It was not an impulsive gesture; there were two reasons for his refusal: objective and personal.

Official honours, he pointed out, he had always declined in the past. He had earlier refused the *Legion d'Honneur* ("Legion of Honour") and not agreed to take a seat in the *College de France*. A writer, Sartre said, who adopts political, social, or literary positions must act only with the means that are his own—that is, the "*written word*". Acceptance of honours has a negative influence on the writer's ability to do this. "*If I sign myself Jean-Paul Sartre,*" he said "*it is not the same thing as signing Jean-Paul Sartre, Nobel Laureate.*"

> *"A writer who accepts an honour involves himself as well as the institution that honours him. My sympathies for the Venezuelan revolutionists commit only myself, while if*

---

[102] "*Sartre on the Nobel Prize*", 'Jean-Paul Sartre', Translated by Richard Howard, New York Reviewer, December, 1964.

Jean-Paul Sartre the Nobel laureate champions the Venezuelan resistance, he also commits the entire Nobel Prize as an institution."

As regards the objective reasons, Sartre said:

> *"The only battle possible today on the cultural front is the battle for peaceful coexistence of two cultures, that of the East and that of the West. The confrontation of these two cultures is inevitable and shall take the form of a conflict— but such confrontation must occur between men and between cultures, without the intervention of institutions. This is why I cannot accept an honour awarded by cultural authorities."*

In case he accepts the prize, he pointed out, the right-wing bloc will interpret it as his subjugation to the bourgeois system. In the same spirit, although all his sympathies were on the socialist side, he would be quite as unable to accept, for example, the Lenin Prize, if someone wanted to give it to him. Nobel Prize, in his opinion he said, though in itself is not a literary prize of the Western bloc, but it stands objectively as a distinction reserved for the writers of the West or the rebels of the East. It has not been awarded to Neruda, one of the greatest South American poets, or to Louis Aragon, though he certainly deserves it. Regrettably, the prize was given to Pasternak, and not to Sholokhov, the only Soviet work honoured is one published abroad and banned in its own country.

Sartre also said he might have considered accepting the prize if it had been awarded in recognition of the action taken by him with a group of 121 writers *("Declaration of the 121")* against French violence in Algeria, *"because it would have honoured not just me, but also the freedom for which we were fighting"*. But matters did not turn out that way, and it is only after the battle was over that the prize has been awarded to him.

Regrets? Well, he had some regret– at least about the money. His principled stand cost him 250,000 kronor (about £21,000), prize money that, he reflected in his refusal statement, he could have donated to the "apartheid committee in London" who badly needed support at the time.

Later, in an interview with Canadian TV in 1976, Sartre said *"To have accepted it [Nobel Prize], would have given me a little badge of distinction, a little symbol of power, which would have separated me, a worker of the mind, from other members of the proletariat".*

Sartre's biographer, Annie Cohen-Solal, interprets Sartre's refusal of the Nobel Prize *"as an attempt to retain ethical purity"*. Behind his refusal, there was profound wish for inviolability and purity. According to her, *"in order to maintain his independence Sartre would not allow himself to be used by any authority whatever."* Pointing out that Sartre was aware that becoming a Nobel Laureate would transform him into an establishment figure which he would have never relished, she said *"Sartre had refused to be embalmed alive, to be made into a living statue and prematurely canonized."* [103]

Sartre's Refusal of Nobel: *Reactions*

The reaction to Sartre's decision not to accept Nobel Prize was mostly negative. Solzhenitsyn reacted with hurt, because Sartre had said in his explanation that the Nobel Prize could have been given to Sholokhov, a writer whom Solzhenitsyn considered to be an "*executioner*". Gabriel Marcel, the noted philosopher, called him a *"systematic blasphemer"*. Surrealist writer, poet Andre Breton saw Sartre's action as a form of *"propaganda"* and opined that Sartre by his refusal had poisoned the very notion of refusal. The Marxist ideologist Kostas Axelos, Professor of Philosophy at Sorbonne, claimed that Sartre would have felt at home under the regimes of both Hitler and Stalin.

---

[103] Cohen-Solal, Annie: *"Sartre: A Life"*, Pantheon, August 12, 1988.

There were also many who considered Sartre's decision as rude and disrespectful of the institution that awards Nobel Prize – the venerable Nobel Institute.

Why Nobel was awarded to Sartre despite his reluctance?

People have wondered why Swedish Academy awarded the Nobel Prize to Sartre though he had intimated the Academy beforehand in writing regarding his inability to accept it.

The Swedish Academy keeps all information about nominations and selections for Nobel Prize secret for 50 years. The details behind Sartre's selection therefore remained hazy and could not be ascertained earlier. The archives have now been opened, and it reveals Sartre's letter dated 16 September 1964 to the committee asking them not to choose him as winner was received at the Academy after the decision had been made.

According to Swedish paper *"Svenska Dagbladet"*, in total, there were 76 nominations that year, of which 19 were new candidates. After detailed deliberations, the jury decided to propose Sartre as their winner on 17 September 1964; other names in the running that year included Russian writer Mikhail Sholokhov, who won the prize the following year, and British poet WH Auden, who never got the award.

Sartre enjoys both the prestige of being offered the Nobel Prize and the dubious distinction rejecting the offer. No one else was offered the prize in his place. Therefore, in the annals of the Swedish Nobel Academy, Sartre is still recorded as the 1964 Nobel Prize winner in Literature. [104][105][106]-------------

---

[104] Richard Howard: *"Sartre on the Nobel Prize – Jean-Paul Sartre"*, (translated into English)), The New York Review of Books, 17 December, 1964

[105] Ursula K Le Guin: "*No Time to Spare: Thinking about what Matters"*, Houghton Mifflin Harcourt, Boston, New York, 2017.

[106] Stralen, Hans van: "C*hoices and Conflict: Essays on Literature and Existentialism"*, P.I.E. - Peter Lang, Presses Interuniversitaires Europeennes, Brussels, 2005.

Chapter 21
Sartre's Lifelong Companion: Simone de Beauvoir

"We were two of a kind, and our relationship would endure as long as we did: but it could not make up entirely for the fleeting riches to be had from encounters with different people."

--- Simone de Beauvoir

Jean-Paul Sartre and Simone de Beauvoir were what kids today might call '*Beyonce-Jay Z*' couple of their times. In 1929, Sartre met Simone in Paris, who studied at Sorbonne and later became a noted philosopher, writer, and feminist. The two became lifelong companions, with a romantic *albeit* open relationship. Both of them joined the French Public Education Service.

Born on January 9, 1908 in Paris, to a respected bourgeois family, Simone's father was a lawyer, her mother a housewife, and together they brought up their two daughters to be progressive, forward-looking and intelligent. De Beauvoir attended the elementary school *Cours Desir* in 1913, but she had no female friends at school. There were only two girl students, both Jewish; of them Simone Weil wanted nothing to do with her, while the other one Georgette Levy lived in the fashionable 16th arrondissement, and the difference in their social background ended what might have been an interesting friendship. Many years later Simone de Beauvoir insisted that she had never been anti-Semitic, but when asked whether her attitude toward Georgette Levy might have been influenced in some way by the harsh antipathy of her own father toward Jews, she said curtly, "Probably."

1929: Simone meets Sartre

"I was intelligent, certainly, but Sartre was a genius."

-- Simone de Beauvoir

After attending the elementary school, de Beauvoir attended the *L'Institute Sainte Nary* under the tutelage of Robert Garric, followed by the *Institute Catholique* in Paris, before finally attending the Sorbonne, where she graduated from in 1929. It was here in her final year she met Sartre, the man who would become her lifelong friend and companion, and had a profound influence on her philosophy of life.

Sartre and Simone met whilst studying for the aggregation in philosophy, the elite French graduate degree. Sartre was 24 and Simone was 21. Of all the students at the Sorbonne, de Beauvoir wrote in her memoirs, *"only Sartre's little band remained closed to me*." She described them with an accurate but a somewhat understatement: *"They had a bad reputation*." Jean-Paul Sartre, Paul Nizan and Rene Maheu, who were officially enrolled in the elite training ground of the intelligentsia, the *Ecole Normale Superieure*, attended lectures only if they liked the professor; otherwise they boycotted their classes. They spoke only to one another and in a kind of code, with private nicknames. They ogled and teased women students and made fun of the men. Worst of all - so went the student gossip - Sartre, the ringleader, the most sarcastic, most brilliant of them all, was a heavy drinker! While the other students went out of their way to avoid this little band, de Beauvoir plotted how to make them notice her so that she could become a part of it.

When they began to study together, de Beauvoir's interest in Sartre was still purely intellectual, judging by her description of the initial impression he made on her: "*I think he was the dirtiest, the most poorly dressed, and I think also the ugliest* [of the three]. I remember seeing him once in the hallways of the Sorbonne: he was wearing an oversized hat and flirting outrageously with some female students. he was really turning on the charm. "

Sartre's associates all knew her - the youngest student in their group, quite possibly the brightest in studies, who was breaking every record for high marks. They also knew her as *"the badly dressed one with the beautiful blue eyes"* and mistook her awkward shyness for an air of superiority that was certainly not the case. So it was a situation in which she and they watched one another surreptitiously, but as the acknowledged rulers of the student society they were not about to make the first move. A standoff of a sort ensued until the next term, when events brought them together.

After her grandfather died in May of 1929, de Beauvoir returned to her classes in a black dress and a hat swathed in black tulle, which made her feel very mysterious and dramatic. On her first day back, she encountered Sartre, Maheu and another student, Pierre Guille, lolling about in a hallway. Later, in class together, ~~he~~ Maheu handed over to her a present from Sartre: a drawing of a man intended to be Leibniz, the subject of her thesis, with representations of the monads (in Leibniz's thought, the essential constituents of the universe) as bathing beauties. More than 50 years later, she recalled in her memoirs how it made her blush.

Although de Beauvoir and Sartre had exchanged greetings once or twice in passing, they had never talked. After Maheu gave her Sartre's drawing, she frequently saw the two of them together, but even though Maheu sometimes spoke to her, she and Sartre still never spoke.

De Beauvoir passed the first examinations brilliantly at the end of May 1929. Now all that stood between herself and her personal freedom was the written examination and, if she passed that, the final oral examination, to be held at the end of June. She was working diligently on her own when, one day in early June, Maheu told her that Sartre had asked to meet her. "*A simple statement, nothing very special,*" she remembered. "*A remark unconnected to anything such as studying together or that he found me attractive and wanted to take me out. Just that Sartre had asked to be introduced to me.*"

Several weeks later, the formal introduction took place in an unusual manner. Sartre's friends had decided to begin joint study sessions to prepare for the oral examinations. To her surprise, de Beauvoir was also invited there in Sartre's room to tell them all that she knew about Leibniz.

> "*I was over the moon,*" she wrote in her memoirs to describe how she felt when he invited her. "*I was so nervous I don't think I slept at all the night before.* [...] *I prepared for the* [...] *study session as if I were going to take the examination itself. I was terrified they would not find me brilliant but only a silly girl who knew very little and could not think.*"

When she arrived at his room, she found the others already gathered. Sartre escorted her to the only chair with great courtesy, and at once they began to work. No sooner had she begun to expound Leibniz's theory than they all decided they knew enough and pronounced her boring, which put an abrupt end to her ostensible reason for being there; nevertheless, no one suggested she leave, and Sartre went out of his way to make her feel welcome. He began to perform, punning and singing philosophical parodies. In her diary and again later in her memoirs, she described her attempts to argue with him and ferret out the weak points of his theories. She claimed that she could never best him, that his thinking was always the most persuasive and his view the one the group always accepted. "*I was intelligent, certainly, but Sartre was a genius.*" [107]

De Beauvoir and Sartre not only passed the crucial examination, they did so with brilliance. Sartre stood first and she came out second in the examination;-moreover, at the age of 21, she also had the distinction to be the youngest person ever to have sat for the examination at the time. The decision to choose between the two was close and it took the committee a long time to make up its mind to give Sartre first place: 'The examiners were so impressed by the precision of de Beauvoir's philosophical expression that they wanted to give her the first place. Finally, they decided to give the first place to Sartre although the examiners were generally of the view that she was, strictly speaking, the better philosopher.

De Beauvoir & Sartre: An open relationship

"What we have is an essential love; but it is a good idea for us also to experience contingent love affairs."

--- Jean-Paul Sartre to Simone de Beauvoir

Between the two, Sartre was the first one to propose. Though de Beauvoir at the time had a boyfriend, but still she fell in love with Sartre owing to his charm and the things they had in common. Both of them were sharp and aspiring, who liked to drink and talk all night. Together, they decided that they would not go in for a traditional marriage, something not acceptable to society at the time.]

[107] Bair, Deirdre: "*How Love Came to Simone de Beauvoir* ", The New York Times", April 8, 1990.

Simone de Beauvoir: The Author of '*The Second Sex*'

The young Sartre already saw himself as a Don Juan, a seducer who ruptured outworn social conventions. Late in life, he admitted that he had fantasised a succession of women for himself, each one meaning everything for a given moment. De Beauvoir had astonished him by agreeing to the experiment he had outlined. She accepted the freedom he insisted on and became its custodian.

"*What we have*," he told young de Beauvoir, "*is an essential love; but it is a good idea for us also to experience contingent love affairs*." His proposal, shocking though it may seem to many others, was apparently quite acceptable to de Beauvoir as she writes: "*We were two of a kind, and our relationship would endure as long as we did: but it could not make up entirely for the fleeting riches to be had from encounters with different people*."

Thus, Sartre and Simone, both, by consent, chose to have a romantic but open relationship for 51 years. They slept together and also had affairs on the side that they would describe to each other in every intimate detail. Together, they challenged the contemporary cultural and social mores.

It is difficult to imagine the sheer adventurousness of this pact forged in 1929. Particularly on de Beauvoir's side, the break from accepted norms was monumental, as was the social stigma. Actually, to her, Sartre seemed to be repeating only what, in bourgeois practice, was always a male prerogative. The only thing that was different in their relationships was that she, the woman, would also be equally free to engage in other affairs. There, too, in Sartre's proposal, there was insistence on the need of "transparency" - the vow that they would never lie to each other the way married couples did. They would tell each other everything, share feelings, work, projects. So, it seemed to be quite a fair proposal to her and there was just no reason not to accept the same.

Yet in their lifelong relationship of supposed equals, he, it turned out, was far more equal than she was. Compared to her, it was Sartre who engaged in countless more affairs. Intriguingly however, they both enjoyed sharing every detail of these escapades. Between the lines of her fiction and what are in effect six volumes of autobiography, it is evident that deep inside de Beauvoir suffered from a kind of discontent and extreme jealousy. She wanted to keep the image of a model life intact. There were no children. They never shared a house and their sexual relations were more or less over by the end of the war, though for much of their life and certainly at the last, they saw each other daily.

Simone de Beauvoir: Mother of Modern Feminism

"One is not born, but rather becomes, a woman."

— Simone de Beauvoir, "The Second Sex"

While Sartre was a great philosopher and a preeminent intellectual, one who popularised '*Existentialism*'. Simone was also an existentialist philosopher and renowned for her role in the feminist movement of the day. After graduating from the Sorbonne, she went on to teach Latin at Lycee Victor Duruy, philosophy at a school in Marseilles, and a few other teaching positions before coming to teach at the Sorbonne for twelve years from 1931 to 1943. In 1943, with the money she had earned from teaching, de Beauvoir turned her full attention to writing, producing first "*L'Envitee*", then "*Pyrrhus et Cineas*" in 1944. In 1945, de Beauvoir and Sartre founded and edited '*Le Temps Modernes*', a monthly review of philosophical thought and trends. In 1948, she wrote perhaps her most famous philosophical work, "*The Ethics of Ambiguity*". In 1949, she wrote "*The Second Sex*", that discussed the treatment of women in the present society as well as down the timeline throughout the history, which is regarded by many as a classic of contemporary feminist literature. Considered the '*mother of modern feminism*', her book created sensation and gave rise to second-wave feminism during the 1960s.

Because of de Beauvoir's stern demeanour and light moustache, Raymond Aron, Friend of both Sartre and de Beauvoir, sarcastically called her *"the father of modern feminism"*. Camus was even less charitable; he found her *"a chatterbox, a blue stocking, unbearable"*.

Sartre & Simone

The English novelist Angela carter was, however, somewhat sympathetic to de Beauvoir; she would ask: *"There is one question that every woman in the western world must have asked herself at one time or another. Why is a nice girl like Simone de Beauvoir sucking up to a boring old fart like Jean-Paul Sartre?"*

Angela Carter

Chapter 22
A close look at Jean-Paul Sartre: The man within

" [....] Had he lived, my father would have laid down on top of me with all his weight and squashed me."

--- Jean-Paul Sartre, 'Les Mots'

Sartre: An "unnatural" childhood

Sartre lost his father when he was just over one year old. Surprisingly, he calls it his "*good fortune*". The result, he said, was that "*I have no superego*."

In his autobiography, *"Les Mots"* (*"The Words", 1964*), commenting on fatherhood and his father, Sartre wrote: *"There is nothing better than to produce children, but what a sin to have some. The death of Jean-Baptiste* [*his father*] *was my greatest piece of good fortune.... Had he lived, my father would have laid down on top of me with all his weight and squashed me.*" [108]

He grew up in the home of his domineering maternal grandfather, Karl "Charles" Schweitzer, uncle of the medical missionary Albert Schweitzer, Nobel Peace Prize winner, and himself a respected writer on topics of religion, philosophy, and languages. There he and her mother were treated as "the children" of the family. Sartre was coddled by his mother, who dressed him like a girl. She was more like his elder sister. Sartre maintained a complicated relationship with his grandfather throughout his

[108] Hayman, Romald, "*Sartre: A Biography*", Da Capo Press, February 14, 1993..

childhood. The young Sartre resented Schweitzer's domineering presence. However, Sartre was receptive to the tutoring of his grandfather, who had recognized early on Sartre's curious, unique mind.

In his autobiography, *Sartre recalls,* in his childhood he, a boy small in stature and cross-eyed, would wander with his mother in the Luxembourg Gardens of Paris, near their home, in search of playmates. They would roam round the park and go from group to group—in the vain hope of being accepted—then finally retreat to the sixth floor of their apartment "*on the heights where* [the] *dreams dwell.*"

Sartre describes in his autobiography, his childhood as "*unnatural*". Forlorn, lacking friends of his own age, he found his companions in books. "*It was in books that I encountered the universe*," he once said. He also began writing when he was a very young boy; he would write for six to seven hours a day and much more. Reading and writing thus became his twin passions. It helped him escape from a world that had rejected him but that he would proceed to rebuild in his own fancy.

When he was 12, his mother remarried; Sartre was devastated. They moved to La Rochelle; his stepfather was an engineer at the local shipyard. There young Sartre suffered under his domineering stepfather, whom he called an "intruder". The experiences shaped his character to rebel against any restriction or domination.

All in all, Sartre's childhood provides a bundle of Freudian clues to his career, (which probably explains why he detested Freud and any suggestion that childhood determines character or the fate of an individual). There, say his biographers, lies the reason for Sartre's interest in the lives of Baudelaire, Flaubert, and Genet. There is Baudelaire's shame and rage at his mother's re-marriage,

Flaubert's feeling of expulsion, Genet's belief that he was rejected by everyone, by life itself.

A man in great hurry

Sartre was a man always in great hurry. He "*resented the time he had to spend on washing, shaving, cleaning his teeth, taking a bath, excreting and he would economise by carrying on conversations through the bathroom door*". ["Les Mots", 1964]

He got the Director of Ecole Normale Supérieure fired from his post

"Only the guy who isn't rowing has time to rock the boat."

-- Jean-Paul Sartre

From his first year at *Ecole Normale Supérieure*, Sartre was a notorious prankster. He liked to shock his fellow students. At one dance, he turned up naked; at a university ball he paraded a hooker in a red dress. In 1927, his antimilitarist satirical cartoon published in the University revue, coauthored with Georges Canguilhem, particularly upset the Director Gustave Lanson. In the same year, he, with his friends, organized a media prank informing the press that Charles Lindbergh, who had at that time shot into fame after his successful New York City–Paris flight, was going to be awarded an honorary École degree. Many newspapers, including '*Le Petit Parisien*', announced the event. Thousands, including journalists and curious spectators, showed up only to find a Lindbergh look-alike presented before them by Sartre and his associates. This caused so much public outcry that Lanson, the Director of Ecole, had to resign from his post.

Professor Gustave Lanson

Café de Flore

"We are completely settled there* [Café de Flore]*; from nine o'clock in the morning until midday, we work, we eat, and at two o'clock we come back and chat with friends until eight o'clock. After dinner, we see people who have an appointment. That may seem strange to you, but we are at home."

--- Jean-Paul Sartre

Hayman's biography describes Sartre as one who *"felt most at home in cafes and restaurants where he could annex space by dominating the conversation and exhaling smoke.* [109]

Sartre, de Beauvoir writes, would fuel himself by a daily intake of between three to four litres of alcohol and coffee, a dozen corydrane tablets, a mixture of amphetamine and aspirin and forty Boyard cigarettes. To Sartre, smoking was *"the symbolic equivalent of destructively appropriating the entire world."*

---

[109] Hayman, Romald, "*Sartre: A Biography*", Da Capo Press, February 14, 1993.

Sartre and de Beauvoir remained regulars at the famous Café de Flore on the Boulevard Saint-Germain in Paris, until the mid-1940s and it is said that Sartre had a special line for his phone calls. The first floor of Le Flore, then, was composed almost entirely of existentialists silently installed to write their respective works. Albert Camus, Raymond Aron, Maurice Merleau-Ponty were regular visitors, too.

Sartre & de Beauvoir at Cafe de Flore, Paris

In 1939, the new manager of the Café de Flore had the brilliant idea of installing a larger and more powerful coal-fired heater and that huge improvement was very popular with the locals who suffered in their freezing apartments, helping Le Flore to become the place to go for poor writers and artists.

Sartre wrote of the Café de Flore, "*We are completely settled there; from nine o'clock in the morning until midday, we work, we eat, and at two o'clock we come back and chat with friends until eight o'clock. After dinner, we see people who have an appointment. That may seem strange to you, but we are at home.*" [110]

Fixated on Crabs

In February, 1935, Sartre entered Sainte-Anne's Hospital in Le Havre, France, and was given an injection of the psychedelic drug mescaline. He was writing a book on 'imagination' and hoped that the drug would induce hallucinations,

The dose he took was too high. He started seeing various sea creatures like octopus, jellyfish, lobsters, and crabs. Even when the drug wore off, he continued hallucinating, seeing lobsters and crabs for several years. Crabs started following him -- everywhere he went, *all the time.*

In an interview with John Gerassi, Professor of Political Science at City University of New York and his long- time friend, Sartre said that the crabs even chased him down the Champs Elysees in Paris once.

> *"They followed me in the streets, into class. I got used to them. I would wake up in the morning and say, 'Good morning, my little ones, how did you sleep?' I would talk to them all the time."*

He thought he was going insane, so he turned to undergo psychoanalysis with none other than his good friend, the noted

---

[110] Jean-Paul Sartre and Simone de Beauvoir acquired their notoriety at the same time that they became "pillars" of the Café de Flore. At the end of the war, the place was transformed into the epicentre of Parisian artistic and intellectual life. It brought together young artists, thinkers and jazz lovers. For some years, Boris Vian, Léo Ferré and Jacques Prévert made the place their home.

French psychiatric and psychoanalyst Jacques Lacan. Together they concluded that the crabs were symbolic of his fear of loneliness.

Jacques Lacan

> *"The crabs stayed with me until the day I simply decided that they bored me and that I just wouldn't pay attention to them. The crabs were mine. I had got used to them. I would have liked my crabs to come back.*"

Sartre's obsession with crabs partially inspired his novel "*Nausea*". Crabs became a recurring motif throughout his writings. Several of his characters compare themselves and their libidos to crabs'. The craziest is Franz, *in Sartre's play "The Condemned in Altona"*, who claims he is being visited by intelligent crabs from the early 30th century who criticize the horrors committed by humanity in the 20th century. [111]

[111] Brookfield, Thomas J. Riedlinger: "*Sartre's Rite of Passage*", The Journal of Transpersonal Psychology, Illinois, Vol.14. No.2, 1982.

Sartre: The Cartoonist

The skill with the pen often moves in unison with a keen visual sense. William Faulkner, for example, created some very fine pen-and-ink illustrations for his college newspaper during his brief time at Ole Miss. Franz Kafka's expressionistic sketches are also quite striking, despite his anguished protestations to the contrary. And Jorge Luis Borges' doodles are as quirky and playful as the author himself. And last but not the least is the great Indian poet and writer Tagore who took up painting relatively late in his career, when he was in his sixties. Nevertheless, he produced thousands of works and was the first Indian artist to exhibit across Europe, Russia and the United States. His painting style was very individual, characterised by simple bold forms and a rhythmic quality. It may, therefore, not be unreasonable to be curious about Sartre's skill as an artist, but here, honestly speaking, it cannot be gainsaid that the great French existentialist philosopher, novelist, and playwright, who was found to have indulged in some occasional sketches, was rather less than accomplished. It's certainly for the best for him that Sartre never quit his day job for an art career.

A caricature drawn by Sartre, titled
"*Le Contentment de soi*"— "Self-Satisfaction"

Sartre's sketches are, ex-facie, rough, childlike caricatures. There is, however, a certain wicked charm in Sartre's visual satires of human moral failings, which he calls a "series de 'douze vices sans allusion'"—roughly, "a series of twelve vices without reference.", although only six sketches are really available, which can be seen in Yale's Beinecke Rare Book & Manuscript Library, which houses these sketches. [112] As for

[112] Either Sartre only completed half the series, or—more likely—half have been lost since the author assures the recipient of his handiwork, a Mademoiselle Suzanne Guille, that he presents to her a "série complete."

Who was Suzanne Guille? Yale's Beinecke Rare Book & Manuscript Library, which houses these sketches, gives us no indication. Perhaps she was a relative, perhaps the spouse, of Pierre Guille, Simon de Beauvoir's last lover? Given the many complicated liaisons pursued by both Sartre and his partner, the possibilities are indeed intriguing.

the drawings? Their subjects hold more interest than their execution, providing us with keys to Sartre's moral universe. [113]

Fond of having a good time

Sartre and de Beauvoir spent a lot of time partying: talking, drinking, dancing, laughing, loving and listening to music with friends. They used to enjoy parties --- the parties were an expression of their philosophy of seizing life, and for them there were authentic and inauthentic ways to do this.

For de Beauvoir in particular, philosophy was to be lived vivaciously, and partying was bound up with her urge to live fully and freely. She wrote that sometimes "[I do] *everything a little too crazily ... But that is my way. I have rather not to do the things at all as doing them mildly.*"

Sartre loved the imaginative playfulness that alcohol facilitated: '*I liked having confused, vaguely questioning ideas that then fell apart.*" Too much seriousness, they felt, hardens the world, pinning it down with rules, suffocating freedom and creativity. A serious party neglects the underlying virtues of playfulness and generosity that make a party authentic. De Beauvoir tried smoking joints but, no matter how hard she inhaled, she remained firmly planted to the ground. She and Sartre self-medicated with amphetamines to remedy hangovers, heartbreaks and writers' blocks. Alcohol was always their drug of choice for partying.

---

113 "*The Drawings of Jean-Paul Sartre*", Open Culture, in Art, Letters, Philosophy, April 21, 2014.

"Hell is – other people!": Not during party time

Although Sartre is renowned for his line '*Hell is – other people*!' in '*No Exit*' (1944), that was far from what he would seek in real life. Both he and de Beauvoir discovered themselves in parties, private or otherwise, in their relations with other people. "*In songs, laughter, dances, eroticism, and drunkenness*," de Beauvoir writes in 'The Ethics of Ambiguity' (1947), "*one seeks both an exaltation of the moment and a complicity with other men*." For her, complicity and reciprocity are the foundation of ethical relationships because other people provide the context of our lives. And because our world is infused with the meanings that other people are giving it, our existence can be revealed only in communication with them. [114]

Sartre & de Beauvoir: It's time for parties

For Sartre and de Beauvoir, parties can cultivate our connections to others, bring meaning to one another's lives, and reveal the world with them. The warmth and laughter that

---

[114] Cleary, Skye C.: "*Being and drunkenness: how to party like an existentialist*", Aeon.

authentic partying sparks can help people cope with the chaos of life. De Beauvoir wrote of her wartime parties in occupied Paris: they saved up food stamps and then binged on food, fun and alcohol. They danced, sang, played music and improvised. The artist Dora Maar mimed bullfights, Sartre mimed orchestra-conducting in a cupboard, and Albert Camus banged on saucepan lids as if in a marching band. De Beauvoir wrote that, '*We merely wanted to snatch a few nuggets of sheer joy from this confusion and intoxicate ourselves with their brightness, in defiance of the disenchantments that lay ahead.*" These were small acts of rebellion in the face of real fears for the future.

Critics of de Beauvoir and Sartre would, however, often try to discredit them with accusations of inspiring orgies, encouraging hedonism, and being what the philosopher Julia Kristeva in 2016 called '*libertarian terrorists*' who formed a '*shock commando unit*' to seduce their sexual victims. For de Beauvoir, there's nothing philosophically wrong with having orgies, it's the same as with any other aspect of life. If a person, she wrote, "*brings his entire self to every situation, there can be no such thing as a 'base occasion'*." And it's true that although de Beauvoir and Sartre had many lovers, casual sex was not a part of their repertoire. They thought that promiscuity was a trivial use of freedom and, instead, indulged in intense love affairs and friendships. An existential approach to partying recognises that although life can be menacing, it can and should be enjoyable, and being with others in the playful mode of partying can help us bear the darkness through a shared sense of euphoria, harmony and hope.

Chapter 23
Sartre: Private Life

"Since it is difficult, or rather impossible, to represent a man's life as entirely spotless and free from blame, we should use the best chapters in it to build up the most complete picture and regard this as the true likeness. Any errors or crimes, on the other hand, which may tarnish a man's career and may have been committed out of passion or political necessity, we should regard rather as a lapse from a particular virtue than as the products of some innate vice. We must not dwell on them too emphatically in our history, but should rather show indulgence to human nature for its inability to produce a character which is absolutely good and uncompromisingly dedicated to virtue"

- Plutarch, The Life of Cimon

Plutarch

Beware

The '*Private life of Jean-Paul Sartre*' depicted in the sections below contains materials that may not be in conformity with the prevailing social norms and may militate against one's sense of morality. Therefore, according to the ethical code laid down for writing history by Plutarch, the great Greek biographer and essayist, occupationally a priest (who worked as a magistrate and an ambassador too), this chapter perhaps should have been omitted. However, for the sake of completeness, we have considered it fit and proper to include these materials, particularly for the benefit of those who don't share the conservatism of Plutarch and wish to know it all. And why not? Plutarch was too conservative. Ain't it? Let's not forget he was a priest after all.

Private Life of Jean-Paul Sartre

"We were two of a kind, and our relationship would endure as long as we did: but it could not make up entirely for the fleeting riches to be had from encounters with different people."

— Simone de Beauvoir, on her relationship with Jean-Paul Sartre

In consonance with his own philosophy of '*freedom*' and '*authentic living*', Sartre freely indulged in uninhibited sex. A grand philanderer, he had many mistresses at a time. Despite his stunted stature and squinted eyes, he was always surrounded by adoring women happy to pamper his genius. Sartre always said the best way to learn about a country was to sleep with its women.

Sartre loved beautiful women, made a hobby of seducing them; but he writes in his letters, he had no more interest in the act of sex than he did in brushing his ruined teeth.

Even at the end, by then he was incontinent, lame and nearly blind, Sartre was surrounded by as many as nine young women, all pouring concern over his health.

Sartre & de Beauvoir: Dangerous liaisons

Sartre and de Beauvoir, the duo had, by consent, a strange romantic but open relationship. Even when Sartre was drafted for World War II, their sex games still continued through letters. Simone, left behind in Paris, would seduce both men and women, and write titillating descriptions of her activities to Sartre.

They were serial seducers bent on their own gratification and as a couple they used their apparently lofty philosophy as a springboard to excuse their multiple liaisons. The underlying truth, however, was that while Simone de Beauvoir preached her ideal of feminist independence and equality, eschewing so-called *'bourgeois'* concepts as marriage and children, and claiming that women should behave just like men, such a lifestyle, scholars and researchers believe, actually made her bitterly unhappy and she became obsessively jealous over Sartre's countless conquests. So, despite her high-flown rhetoric, it was only for revenge and out of frustration that she embarked on affairs, always secretly hoping they would provoke Sartre to return to her. [115]

Astonishingly, it was her craven desire to please Sartre that led de Beauvoir to groom young female lovers for him, commonly girls she had bedded herself. De Beauvoir was a bi-sexual; there were many allegations against her of sexually exploiting and abusing her young girl students. She was also the procuress, mostly her teenager pupils, for Sartre's enjoyment in which she would often participate. At times she would also mock those pupils in her letters to Sartre.

---

[115] Roberts, Glenys: "*Dangerous liaisons and sex with teens: The story of Satire and de Beauvoir as never told before*", MailOnline, 12 April 2008.

A Disgraceful Affair

Her former 16-year-old student *Binaca Lamblin* (originally 'Bianca Bienenfeld'), who was 14 years her junior, has narrated in her book *"A Disgraceful Affair"*, how she was sexually exploited and abused by both Sartre and her teacher de Beauvoir. Soon after she was seduced by her teacher, de Beauvoir introduced her lover to Sartre. He promptly made it his mission to seduce Bienenfeld. After a romantic entanglement between the three of them, de Beauvoir told Sartre to end it, which he abruptly did in a letter.

Bienenfeld's book also describes how at the onset of World War II, the duo promptly abandoned her, as she was a Jew, for which she nearly lost her life at the hands of the Nazis who were then advancing on Paris. [116]

When she read "*Letters to Sartre*" and saw the flippant tone the pair took toward her, she said, "*Their perversity was carefully concealed beneath Sartre's meek and mild exterior and the Beaver's serious and austere appearance. In fact, they were acting out a commonplace version of 'Dangerous Liaisons.'*" [117]

Sartre: A Serial Seducer

And the 16-year-old Bienenfeld is not the only instance of their extreme sexual escapades. Sartre tended to treat younger romantic prospects (all of whom were female) more as conquests than partners, spending months or years persuading them to get into bed with him and then bouncing off to regale "*the Beaver*" with details.

---

[116] Lamblin, Bianca & Plovnick, Julie (Translator): "*A Disgraceful Affair: Simone de Beauvoir, Jean-Paul Sartre, and Bianca Lamblin*", Women's Life Writings from Around the World, Northeaster University Press, January 1, 1993.

[117] Brown, Hannah: "*Simone de Beauvoir and Jean-Paul Sartre: An Existential Love Story*", Literary Ladies' Guide, An Archive Dedicated to Classic Women Authors and their work, July 26, 2018 | Updated December 3, 2020.

Sartre would pay his mistresses' rent to ensure they were nearby while trying to keep them ignorant of each other. De Beauvoir was sometimes among the deceived, but at other times she was his accomplice in deception.

Interestingly, Sartre also wanted a change of law to suit his lifestyle. So, in 1977, he, along with de Beauvoir, Ronald Barthes, Michel Foucault, Jacques Derrida, child psychologist Françoise Dolto, writers Philippe Sollers, Alain Robbe-Grillet, Louis Aragon and several others of the era's intelligentsia signed a petition seeking to abrogate the age of consent and decriminalisation of paedophilia in France. [118][119]

1943: De Beauvoir loses her job

In 1943, de Beauvoir was removed from her academic job and her teaching licence was permanently revoked on the charge of seducing her 17-year-old lycée pupil *Natalie Sorokine* in 1939. [120][121]

With the posthumous publication in 1988 of de Beauvoir's letters to Sartre, a good proportion of them written during the war years when Sartre was at the front and then a prisoner, gaps that were left out of his autobiography are filled in. What the letters express is not only de Beauvoir's overarching love for a man who is never sexually faithful to her, a man she addresses as her "dear little being" and whose work she loyally edits. They also underline how

---

[118] Krizman, Lawrence D. (Ed.): "*Sexual Morality and the Law*", Chapter 16 "Politics, Philosophy, Culture: Interviews and Other Writings 1977-1984, New York/London: 1990, Routledge, p. 275.

[119] Henley, Jon: "*Calls for legal child sex rebound on luminaries of May 68*", The Guardian. Retrieved February 23, 2001.

[120] Carole Seymour-Jones: "*A Dangerous Liaison: Simone de Beauvoir and Jean-Paul Sartre*", Random House 2011.

[121] Deirdre, Bair: *Simon de Beauvoir A Biography*", Simon &Schuster, 1991.

casually she accommodated his wishes, and consented to what many women would reject as demeaning, utterly unacceptable. [122]

De Beauvoir: Her "beloved husband"

"What an odd thing a diary is: the things you omit are more important than those you put in."

— Simone de Beauvoir, "The Woman Destroyed"

Their relationship was open. They were free to live their own life. Still de Beauvoir, the iconic firebrand feminist, was emotionally at Sartre's beck and call. She craved for his attention. The reverse was not so apparent. Sartre would often have his flings keeping Simone totally in the dark.

To take revenge on Sartre, de Beauvoir, during her US tour in 1947, fell into bed with the Chicago writer Nelson Algren and intimated Sartre of the details of her new relationship. She longed Sartre would insist on her immediate return to Paris. But Sartre told her to stay back in America; for by then he had found a new love – Dolores Vanetti. De Beauvoir, on her part, also shared a decade of transatlantic love letters with Algren, addressing him as her "*beloved husband*." He was a thinly veiled character in her 1954 novel, '*The Mandarins*'.

"You are my destiny": de Beauvoir's mad passion for young lover, 18 Junior to her

De Beauvoir also lived with Claude Lanzmann, a French filmmaker, for the bulk of the 1950s. A letter published recently in

---

[122] Appignanesi, Lisa: "*Did Simone de Beauvoir's open 'marriage' make her happy?*", The Guardian, 10 Jun 2005.

January 2018 reveals her "mad passion" for Lanzmann who was 18 years junior to her. Lanzmann was 26 and Sartre's secretary when the pair met. De Beauvoir was 44. The letter also shows that she was never sexually satisfied by her partner, her life-long companion Jean-Paul Sartre.

The writer of the letter, who condemned marriage as an "*obscene*" institution that enslaved women in her classic book '*The Second Sex*', wrote to Lanzmann in 1953 saying she would throw herself into his "*arms and I will stay there forever. I am your wife forever.*"

In the above letter published by *Le Monde*, de Beauvoir also wrote:

> "*My darling child, you are my first absolute love, the one that only happens once (in life) or maybe never.*
>
> *I thought I would never say the words that now come naturally to me when I see you – I adore you. I adore you with all my body and soul ... You are my destiny, my eternity, my life.*"

The note is one of 112 love letters written by her to Lanzmann, the only man De Beauvoir ever lived with, which has been bought by Yale University. It reveals that Sartre – who had many other lovers and always kept a separate apartment – was never able to satisfy her physically in the same way.

"*I loved him for sure,*" she wrote to Lanzmann, "*but without it being returned – our bodies were for nothing.*"

Nor did she find the same bliss with the American novelist Nelson Algren, author of The Man with the Golden Arm. "*I loved him because of the love he had for me, without any real intimacy and without ever giving to him from inside of myself,*" she added. [123]

The Ultimate Betrayal

So this is what their relationship was like. An open life-long companionship with full liberty to be unfaithful to each other. And apparently it suited them well too. But, it was towards the end, Sartre shattered de Beauvoir in a way she could have never imagined.

The couple had no children as they never wanted children; it had been part of their creed. By the mid-60's, there was apparently some rift in their relationship. Though they continued to stick together, Sartre wanted to cut her off from any access to the huge royalties from his lifetime writings. In 1965, Sartre adopted his 25-year-old Algerian Arlette El-Kaim as his daughter, making her automatically his sole heir when he died. Arlette was Sartre's mistress before adoption.

For de Beauvoir, it was the ultimate betrayal; for now she would no longer be in exclusive control of Sartre's posthumous reputation. Not to be outdone, De Beauvoir also adopted a young girl, Sylvie Le Bon, her pupil aged 16, who inherited her estate in 1986 after her death.

So, de Beauvoir & Sartre – they by mutual consent ignored the traditional marriage as an institution and instead chose to have a romantic but open relationship with liberty to indulge in affairs at will and to share the details of their sexual escapades between themselves later for pleasure.

By Sartre's theory of existentialism, they were "*condemned to be free*". The duo chose their 'freedom' in the manner they

---

[123]Agence France-Presse: "*You are my destiny": Simone de Beauvoir's mad passion for young lover revealed in letters*", The Guardian, 22 January, 2018.

considered it the best. Going by the contemporary social mores, and even by the present-day societal norms, their lifestyle was certainly unusual and would raise a number of questions Were they weird? Were they iconic but flawed? Perverted or were they ahead of their time? But perhaps the most important question among the many questions it raises is what de Beauvoir herself raised in her life and writing: '*When free of gendered and oppressive social expectations, what does love look like*'?

Chapter 24
Sartre on God

"I do not feel that I am the product of chance, a speck of dust in the universe, but someone who was expected, prepared, prefigured. In short, a being whom only a Creator could put here; and this idea of a creating hand refers to God."

--- Jean-Paul Sartre before his death

The basis of Sartre's existentialism is that man must recognise there is no god. Sartre was arguably one of the world's most confirmed atheists. Surprisingly, on the brink of his death in 1980, Sartre showed an interest in Judaism.

Sartre called himself a "material" atheist, one who not only believes that god does not exist but is profoundly aware of god's absence. For Sartre, god's absence is to be felt everywhere. God is missing. And since god is missing, we are to feel the obligation to create ourselves in freedom. [124]

There is a general belief that Sartre was an atheist right from the beginning; but the fact is that he was extremely confused about his religious beliefs right from his childhood. He was religiously vulnerable and spiritually susceptible. In most of his writings, such as, *'Nausea'*, *'The Wall'*, *'Existentialism is humanism'*, *'Being and Nothingness'*, *'The Reprieve'*, *'The Age of Reason,'* to name but a few, there is an excessive atavistic antagonism towards god, which prompted Camus to comment in '*Le Monde*' in 1949,

---

[124] Gellman, Jerome: "*Jean-Paul Sartre: The Mystical Atheist*", European Journal for Philosophy of Religion 2 (2009), pp. 127–137.

> "*To me, Sartre's excessively rabid stand against god is an ontological proof of his deep-down faith in some creator. The man* [Sartre] *is a closet believer who'll die not as an atheist but as a believer.*" So prophetic!

According to Tom Flanley of Cambridge University, Sartre suffered from *'Excess Reverse Syndrome'* (ERS). Where there's excessive hatred, there's love lurking somewhere. What we deny all the time is actually our subconscious belief that's fighting to come out as our faith. To deny is to accept unwittingly. This happened to Sartre. He kept condemning God but god resided in the crevices of his mind. On the contrary, Camus didn't bother about the existence or non-existence of god. God was a non-entity to him. Thus, in all his writings *'The Stranger'*, *'The Plague'*, *'The Myth of Sisyphus'*, *'The Fall'*, *'The Rebel'*, *'The Happy Death'*, *'The Guest*,' et. al., God is a maginalised entity that seldom appears as a character or a metaphor. To quote Camus in '*Le Parisien*' (1953),

> "*I'm theologically indifferent to god and religion and spiritually casual about any esoteric belief(s). I've no time to think or condemn god.*"

But this wasn't the case with Sartre. He was obsessed with the 'non-existence' of god. It was a pathological negation of god that was bound to recoil and re-blossom into equally strong faith in god. Perhaps that's why he called out to a priest just prior to his death.

Sartre: The Mystical Atheist

God has been controversial in Sartre's writings. The 1991 publication of '*L'Espoir maintenant*' reawakened the controversy surrounding Sartre's beliefs just before his death, caused by the dialogue with his friend and Secretary Benny Levy published in '*Le Nouvel Observateur*' (1980). The publication of the translation 'Hope Now', in 1996 re-ignited it inspiring an article by Shlomic

Schuster [125] and a 1997 NASS (North American Sartre Society) conference symposium. The papers vigorously debated the significance and authenticity of Sartre's thinking. The initial controversy was whether Sartre had really recanted his aesthetic faith and whether, as the '*Les Temp modernes*' group believed, he had been intellectually and spiritually abducted, at a time of declining health. Whether being influenced by a number of Jewish thinkers, including Sartre's adopted daughter Arlette El-Kaim, and his friend & the radical revolutionary turned orthodox Jew, Benny Levy, he moved towards theism. Also, even if he was uninfluenced, the question remains, whether he was seduced by monotheism (Judaism), by the enticement of direct relations with an infinite god and a moral code based on a metaphysical absolute?

According to Gellman, whether Sartre had changed his mind or not, the content of *'L'Espoir maintenan*t' is unsurprising since he engaged with god throughout his life.

My God died young: Sartre

Sartre's early life is revealing. He was brought up in a religious household (protestant through his grandfather and Catholic through his mother and Grandmother); his mother and grandmother often took him to the Church for the beautiful music, but there is no evidence that he or his family enjoyed a personal spiritual relationship with god, nor of sincere communal religious practices. In '*Les Mots*' ['Words'], he described his faith as '*La religion bourgeoise*' (bourgeois religion) which, liberal and secular in tone, emphasised the aesthetic and cultural aspects of Christianity. His mother's religion, according to him, was "*a vague religiosity that*

[125] Schuster, Shlomic C.: "*Revisiting 'Hope Now' with Benny Levy: A note on the 1996 English Edition*", Sartre Studies International 4, no. 1 (1998), pp. 63-75.

consoles her a little when she needs it and, the rest of the time, leaves her very much at peace." [126]

Sartre learnt the basics of the faith, but it remained external to him. In his own words, "*I don't think that I ever believed very strongly*". Early in his autography "*Les Mots*" ('The Words'), he recounts his initial encounter with God when he writes that "*as a boy I needed a Creator; I was given a big boss.*"

His mother made him take his first communion without him having any true conviction. God was marginalised. For the young Sartre "*There is not much to be said. God existed, but I didn't bother with him at all.*"

And even this 'little faith' whatever he had in god, disappeared soon, at the age of 12.

> *"One morning in 1917 in La Rochelle, I was waiting for some friends who were going with me to school; they were late and I soon ran out of the things to pass the time, so I decided to think about the Almighty. Immediately he tumbled down out of the sky and disappeared without giving any explanation; I don't know where the thought came from or how it struck me, yet all at once I said to myself, "God doesn't exist." .... "He doesn't exist," I said to myself in polite astonishment, and I thought the matter done and dusted. In a way it was, for since then I have never had the slightest temptation to bring it up again.*
>
> ['*Les Mots*'][127]

---

126 Schuster, Shlomic C.: "*Revisiting 'Hope Now' with Benny Levy: A note on the 1996 English Edition*", Sartre Studies International 4, no. 1 (1998), p. 71.

127 Sartre tells this story to de Beauvoir, which appears in a slightly different version in the autobiography of his youth, "*Les Mots*" ('The Words').

So, just at the age of 12, Sartre lost whatever little faith he had in god.

> For him, he wrote, "*This was an authentic piece of evidence. Though I do not really know on which it was based. And then it was over; I never thought about it again. I bothered no more about this dead God than I had done with the living one. I think it would be hard to find a less religious nature than mine. I sorted out the question once and for all at the age of twelve.*"
>
> [*'Les Mots'*]

Sartre calls this realization an "*intuition*", and later wrote that god's non-existence had become "*manifest*" to him at that moment.

So, for Jean-Paul Sartre, the 'Almighty' god was dead. And He had died young, even before he (Sartre) reached his teens.

The 'Death of God' in Sartre's creative works

"Nothing happens while you live. The scenery changes, people come in and go out, that's all. There are no beginnings. Days are tacked on to days without rhyme or reason, an interminable, monotonous addition."

- Jean-Paul Sartre, "Nausea"

'Nausea'

Given this backdrop, Sartre's atheism, to many, may seem to be the result of a flippant childhood whim. But that would be a mistake. Instead, as Gellman suggests, Sartre possibly had an early serious intuition that led him to his own brand of mystical experience, just as mystical intuition leads the theistic mystic to experience god as the ground of his being. But Sartre's mysticism is not theistic atheism. Sartre was an atheistic mystic. [128]

In '*Les Mots*' ['The Words'], Sartre writes of his first major work '*Nausea'* and its central character Antoine Roquentin:

> "*At the age of thirty, I executed the masterstroke of writing Nausea.... I was Roquentin; I used him to show, without complacency, the texture of my life.*" (pp. 157-158). [129]

In the novel '*Nausea'*, Sartre tells the story of the existential travails of Antoine Roquentin, a young man, a writer, who resides temporarily in a small French town. Roquentin's story revolves around the meaning, or lack of it, he finds in the historical research he is engaged in. The central event of the novel takes place in a park that Roquentin visits from time to time. Here, looking at a chestnut tree, Roquentin has an experience he never had before. Here are some excerpts:

> "*(1) And suddenly, suddenly, the veil is torn away, I have understood, I have seen.* (p. 170*)*
>
> *(2) And then all of a sudden, there it was, clear as day: existence had suddenly unveiled itself. It had lost the harmless look of an abstract category: it was the very paste of things; this root was kneaded into existence. Or rather the root, the park gates, the bench, the sparse grass, all that had vanished: the diversity of things, their individuality, were only an appearance, a veneer. This veneer had melted, leaving soft, monstrous masses, all in disorder—naked, in a frightful, obscene nakedness.* (pp. 171-72)

---

128 Gellman, Jerome: "*Jean-Paul Sartre: The Mystical Atheist*", European Journal for Philosophy of Religion 2 (2009), p. 133..

129 All quotations are from Jean-Paul Sartre, *Nausea*, trans. Lloyd Alexander (New York: New Directions Publishing Company, 1964).

(3) And without formulating anything clearly, I understood that I had found the key to Existence.... In fact, all that I could grasp beyond that returns to this fundamental absurdity. Absurdity: another word; I struggle against words. (p. 173)

(4) This moment was extraordinary. I was there, motionless and icy, plunged in a horrible ecstasy. But something fresh had just appeared in the very heart of this ecstasy. The essential thing is contingency. I mean that one cannot define existence as necessity. To exist is simply to be there...

. I believe there are people who have understood this. Only they tried to overcome this contingency by inventing a necessary, causal being. But no necessary being can explain existence: contingency is not a delusion, a probability which can be dissipated; it is the absolute, consequently, the perfect free gift. (p. 177)

(5) I was the root of the chestnut tree. Or rather I was entirely conscious of its existence. Still detached from it—since I was conscious of it—yet lost in it, nothing but it. (p. 177)

(6) I knew it was the World, the naked World suddenly revealing itself, and I choked with rage at this gross, absurd being." (p. 178)

It needs no emphasis to note that these are all typical instances of mystical experiences. The veil is suddenly lifted, as one sees, an enormous truth is revealed, and one has discovered the key to Existence, the absolute, one cannot move; there is ecstasy, things flow into one another, what one is experiencing is ineffable, there is talk of essential reality, the dissolution of the self into the content of the experience, and so on. [130]

Again, compare Sartre's description of Roquentin's experience to some of the expressions in the following theistic mystical experience:

> "*I remember the night, and almost the very spot on the hilltop, where my soul opened out, as it were, into the Infinite, and there was a rushing together of the two worlds, the inner and the outer.... I stood alone with Him who had made me, and all the beauty of the world, and love, and sorrow, and even temptation. I did not seek Him, but felt the perfect unison of my spirit with His, The ordinary sense of things around me faded. For the moment nothing but an ineffable joy and exultation remained. It is impossible fully to describe the experience. It was like the effect of some great orchestra when all the separate notes have melted into one swelling harmony that leaves the listener conscious of nothing save that his soul is being wafted upwards, and almost bursting with its own emotion. The perfect stillness of the night was thrilled by a more solemn silence, The darkness held a presence that was all the more felt because it was not seen, I could not any more have doubted that He was there than that I was. Indeed, I felt myself to be, if possible, the less real of the two*".

Roquentin's, therefore, was a unitive experience, in which distinctions blurred. His mystical experience is an embryonic instance of an unconstructed awareness - distinctions becoming elusive to the point of disappearing, as in Roquentin's saying that he was the chestnut tree. And from the nature of this mystical

---

[130] Gellman, Jerome: "*Jean-Paul Sartre: The Mystical Atheist*", European Journal for Philosophy of Religion 2 (2009), pp. 134-135.

experience Roquentin comes to know that there is no God. He has seen that reality has no character, no structure, no intrinsic meaning. But if there were a god, reality would have character, structure, and intrinsic meaning. So, by experience Sartre now knows that god is missing in the world, knows god's absence. No wonder that Sartre says of his writing of '*Nausea*', "*As a mystic, I attempted to reveal the silence of being by a thwarted rustling of words….*" (p. 157) [131]

Sartre's deepest atheistic inclinations are, therefore, not those of a philosopher or even those of an existentialist. They are those of a mystic.

"The Flies"

"The first crime was mine: I committed it when I made man mortal. Once I had done that, what was left for you, poor human murderers, to do? To kill your victims? But they already had the seed of death in them; all you could do was to hasten its fruition by a year or two."

- Jean-Paul Sartre, "The Flies"

The death of god has also figured as a dominant theme in Sartre's other theoretical as well as creative works, such as his book "*Being and Nothingness*", published in 1943, and "*The Flies*", a play that was produced in the same year. In fact, the concept that the god is dead constitutes the cornerstone of his philosophical views of Existentialism, nihilism, freedom, and responsibility.

It is hard to understand Sartre's play '*The Flies*' and its philosophical background without considering the concept of the death of god It contends that god is dead and has nothing to do with people's life or prosperity. It shows how the belief in the death of

[131] Ibid., 136.

god may function as a productive force in humans' life and existence.

Existentialism is concerned with the existence of individuals: what they choose, how they act, and what they make of themselves. Such an emphasis on humans indicates the absence of the role of god, something that Existentialists call ‘the death of god’. Existentialism focuses on humans and ignores god, which suggests that the existential belief in the nonexistence of god does not necessarily stem from atheism. While some Existentialists do not believe in the existence of a divine being that has created all other beings and that is able to control all creatures, others like Sartre do not completely deny the existence of god as a creator but believe he does not have roles to play in people's lives anymore. This implies that the concept of the death of god is associated with the idea that life's meanings and values are derived from god's rules.

Sartre's notion of the death of god thus implies the belief in the non-existence of the ‘role’ of god rather than the belief in the non-existence of god, the creator. This notion, as displayed in his 1943-play ‘*The Flies*’, suggests that humans are free and that their will and power should not be restricted by any conjectural conceptions. The death of god, for Sartre, involves the absence of god's role and value from people's life, which entails that humans are fully responsible for their decisions and deeds. Such responsibility may be tiresome as it integrates feelings of hesitation, regret, and despair; yet, it is productive as it grants humans the full freedom to decide and act. Accordingly, Sartre's notion of the death of god is optimistic. It views humans as independent, fully free, and able to conduct whatever desirable for them regardless of whether gods like it.

This viewpoint disagrees with the dominant belief that Existentialism is a pessimistic approach in which the death of god entails nothingness and nihilism. In fact, Sartre's ‘*The Flies*’ suggests that believing in the role or value of god may function as a source of people's misery and nothingness. Sartre views nothingness as a productive force of humans' life. The meaninglessness of life, for Sartre, does not mean that individuals live in despair due to the loss of values and meanings; rather, it suggests that individuals are fully free and responsible for finding and creating their own meanings and values. In '*The Flies*' (1989), people of Argos live in misery and suffer meaninglessness since they are controlled by the King and Queen and due to their belief in the existence of god. They worship Zeus and believe that they will get punished by that deity if they try to rebel against god's rules by living freely. On the contrary, Electra and Orestes escape that bleak atmosphere by rebelling against Zeus through denying his significance and insulting his status. In a nutshell, '*The Flies*' expresses Sartre's belief that nothingness and meaninglessness are the main source of people's freedom and prosperity, which proves that Sartre's belief in the death of god constitutes the backbone of his optimistic Existentialism. [132]

Return of the Dead [God]: *Sartre tilts towards Judaism*

For one like Sartre, known to have lived and believed in a godless world throughout his life, it was no wonder that the news of his inclination towards a monotheism (Judaism) towards the end of his life would create a sensation. Interestingly, the one who revealed Sartre's astonishing change was his friend and ex-Maoist, Pierre Victor (aka Benny Levy), who spent much of his time with the dying Sartre and interviewed him on several of his views. As said by Levy, Sartre had a drastic change of mind about the existence of

[132] Zuraikat, Malek J. & Mashreqi, Sarah: "*The Death of God in Sartre's The Flies*", Acta Scientiarum. Language and Culture, vol. 42, No. 2, Universidade Estadual de Maringá, 2020.

god and started gravitating toward Messianic Judaism. According to Levy, Sartre told him before his death: [133]

> *"I do not feel that I am the product of chance, a speck of dust in the universe, but someone who was expected, prepared, prefigured. In short, a being whom only a Creator could put here; and this idea of a creating hand refers to God."*

Sartre's followers were upset; they could hardly believe it. It would be a clear rejection of Marxism, which is a central theme of Sartre's philosophical thought.

To the dismay of his followers, Sartre confirmed that Levy's interviews were authentic. However he did not consider himself a Jew; he said he was just curious.

De Beauvoir was appalled. Incredible, it seemed to her. Is it not he who said *"The absence of God is more divine than God"*? To allow 'God' now to enter their godless world would be 'blasphemy'; contrary to the philosophy they preached and practised all their lives.

A month later, Sartre died.

Later, de Beauvoir when asked to comment on Sartre's intent to convert to Judaism, expressed her anguish and said:

> *"How should one explain this senile act of a turncoat?"* [134]

----

[133] Paul Sumit: "*Why did Jean-Paul Sartre turn a believer prior to his death*?", The Milli Gazette, 20 June, 2018.

[134] Palau, Luis: "God Is Relevant: Finding Strength and Peace in Today's World", Multnomah, 1998.

Chapter 25
Sartre on Death

"Death is in no way an ontological structure of my being, at least not in so far as my being is for itself; it is the Other who is mortal in his being. There is no place for death in being-for-itself; it can neither wait for death nor realize it nor project itself toward it; death is in no way the foundation of the finitude of the for-itself."

--- Jean-Paul Sartre, 'Being and Nothingness'

Sartre on Death in "Being and Nothingness"

In "*Being and Nothingness*", Sartre criticizes Heidegger's conception of death in "*Being and Time*" and offers his own account of the finitude of existence, which is grounded not in the certainty of death, but rather in our choices and freedom. Since Sartre himself acknowledges that his views on death are supposed to oppose and argue against Heidegger's conception of death in *Being and Time*, it should be mentioned, from the beginning, that there are multiple critiques directed to Sartre's reading of Heidegger that argue that Sartre's views are merely existentialist misinterpretations of Heidegger regarding the place of the subject in philosophy, the distinctions on which Heidegger bases his conception death, and what Heidegger means by "*being-toward-death*".

For instance, Sartre considers subjectivity to be the ground from out of which any philosophizing-thinking should arise, and hence thinks that Heidegger's questioning is problematic, for it is, from the start, endeavours to avoid, or not to pass through, the Cartesian cogito [135].

Another critique directed to Sartre's interpretation of Heidegger is that Sartre overlooks and misreads Heidegger's conception of death and especially Heidegger's distinction between "perishing", "demise", and "being-toward-death".

Although such critiques and arguments are important and justified, Sartre's views on death, as we will see later, certainly deepen, add to, and render richer any attempt at understanding death from out of life or within life.

Death is merely a 'given'

Sartre sees death as "*nothing but a certain aspect of facticity and of being-for-others*" and as "*nothing other than the given*". This means that, for Sartre, one's death is only to a small extent related to one's life and hence it "*is not an ontological structure*" of one's being:

> "*Death is in no way an ontological structure of my being, at least not in so far as my being is for itself; it is the Other who is mortal in his being. There is no place for death in being-for-itself; it can neither wait for death nor realize it nor project itself toward it; death is in no way the foundation of the finitude of the for-itself. In a general way death can neither be founded from within like the project of original freedom, nor can it be received from the outside as a quality by the for-itself. What then is death? Nothing but a certain aspect of facticity and of being-for-others—i.e.,*

135 "*cogito, ergo sum*", (Latin: "*I think, therefore I am*) dictum coined by the French mathematician and philosopher René Descartes in his "*Discourse on Method*" (1637) as a first step in demonstrating the attainability of certain knowledge. It is the only statement to survive the test of his methodic doubt.

nothing other than the given. It is absurd that we are born; it is absurd that we die."

--- Jean-Paul Sartre, 'Being and Nothingness'

Seeing death as merely a "given" does not change the relation into which humans and death are always placed, that is, the finitude of humans. Humans, for Sartre, are finite beings, yet what renders this finitude possible in the first place and constantly confirms it is not a death awaiting and happening in the future, but rather the limitedness pertaining to the present regarding the individual's need to choose a certain project, that is, the limitedness belonging to the need to choose and hence to act in accordance with this choice.

For Sartre, finitude originally arises from, and is first made possible because of the temporal inevitability of pursuing a specific project before another and, at the same time, the impossibility of reversing or changing this sequence of projecting, this order of choosing. Seeing finitude not as a death that awaits and takes place in the future, but rather as what constraints and renders limited the projecting belonging to and happening in the present is a critique directed to Heidegger's conception of death in '*Being and Time*' and an attempt at arguing for both the radical freedom lying at the heart of our being and the distance separating death from life, the distance that renders death not important to life, the distance that renders death meaninglessness.

Death is Meaningless

Sartre argues against Heidegger's view that no one else can die for me by saying that no one else can also love for me. In fact, Sartre says, it is not only loving or dying that no one else can do for me, there are many other things in the world that no one else can do for me.

Sartre also says that death can neither individualize nor be awaited and that one cannot experience one's own death, for if one dies, then nothing remains to be experienced. That is, every experiencing and all experiences disappear when one dies and ceases to exist. Hence, according to Sartre, any attempt at linking oneself together with one's death, that is, any attempt at seeing one's death within one's life is nothing but an attempt at viewing oneself through the eyes of other, through the point of view of the other and nothing more.

Since Sartre, arguing against Heidegger's views in *Being and Time*, thinks that death cannot be experienced by oneself or within one's life, death becomes in the existentialism of Sartre nothing but a contingent fact, which is meaningless and has no meaning to one's life or oneself.

Death renders life Meaningless

Sartre links together the existentialist notion of the absurd with death and thus sees death as what deprives life of meaning and meaningfulness. According to Sartre, death removes and takes away meaning from life, leaves it empty and hollowed out, and hence renders it meaningless.

Death renders life meaningless and senseless, since it is itself meaningless and senseless. Since death renders life meaningless and is itself meaningless and senseless, it cannot be considered to be the completion of life, for it cannot be freely decided or determined within life, that is, from out of one's life.

In fine, death is meaningless and brings about meaninglessness and senselessness. It is radically impersonal and thus it cannot individualize; It cannot be awaited, for if death is to be awaited, it will disrupt and disturb the individual's whole projects, since this awaiting is itself a project, the project of not having a project or the project of the impossibility of projecting.

Death is not different from Birth

Sartre disagrees with Heidegger's view that death shapes *Dasein's* [136] "*being-in-the-world*" toward its future as "*being-toward-death*", and says that death does not belong to life and cannot be thought from out of one's life; death is outside of life and comes from the outside.

Thus, there is nothing that can be done about one's death; it cannot be awaited and it cannot be considered to be one of one's possibilities. Death is nothing but a fact, a mere fact in one's life, in the life of the other; a fact that cannot be distinguished from birth.

> "*We must conclude in opposition to Heidegger that death, far from being my peculiar possibility, is a contingent fact which as such on principle escapes me and originally belongs to my facticity. I can neither discover my death nor wait for it nor adopt an attitude toward it, for it is that which is revealed as undiscoverable, that which disarms all waiting, that which slips into all attitudes (and particularly into those which are assumed with respect to death) so as to transform them into externalized and fixed conducts whose meaning is forever entrusted to others and not to ourselves, Death is a pure fact as is birth; it comes to us from outside and it transforms us into the outside. At bottom it is in no way distinguished from birth, and it is the identity of birth and death that we call facticity.*"
>
> -- Jean-Paul Sartre, '*Being and Nothingness*' [137]

----

[136] *Dasein*, (German: literally, "being there") in the ontology and metaphysics of the German existentialist philosopher Martin Heidegger (1889–1976), the form of Being or existence of the human individual.

[137] "*Sartre on Death in Being and Nothingness*", that-which: Philosophy | Philosophemes | Philosophers.

Chapter 26
Death of Jean-Paul Sartre

"I think of death only with tranquillity, as an end. I refuse to let death hamper life. Death must enter life only to define it."

-- Jean-Paul Sartre, "No Exit"

By 1975, Sartre's health had considerably deteriorated, because of the pressure of work he underwent in course of writing of a massive 2,988-page biography of the great French 19th-century novelist Gustave Flaubert. Sartre had spent two decades studying the author of *Madame Bovary*. In one of his interviews, Sartre admitted he began by regarding Flaubert as the worst example of a bourgeois writer, with no "political engagement". He later came to regard Flaubert's famously disengaged style as a sign of "*maddening artistry: an artistry that was beyond his own talents*".

The magnum opus, he was working on, however, remained unfinished; he stopped writing in 1975 because of failing eyesight. "*I walk a bit,*" he told an interviewer in the year he stopped. "*I have the newspapers read to me, I listen to the radio, I try to make out what's happening on the television screen -- all time-killing activities. The sole object of my life was to write.*" [138]

The incomplete work, "*The Family Idiot*", was published only after Sartre's death

[138] McLellan, Joseph: "*Jean-Paul Sartre, Existential Author, Dramatist, Dies*", The Washington Post, 16 April, 2010.

Apart from the pressure of work, the other factors that majorly contributed to his death were that he was a regular drug user and a notorious chain smoker. His biographer Annie Cohen–Solal writes:

> *"Sartre's daily drug consumption was two packs of cigarettes, several tobacco pipes, over a quart of alcohol, two hundred milligrams of amphetamines, and a load of barbiturates. These had assaulted his system and led to deterioration of his health."*

In his final years, Sartre became a virtual recluse in his small apartment on the in the Montparnasse section on the Left Bank of Paris, but he still acted as a sort of godfather to small, radical student revolutionary movements and sometimes served as titular editor of their newspapers. In the small apartment he lived in, he had very few possessions other than his books which were his constant companions. His gradual loss of sight--he was virtually blind at his death--and failing health slowly forced him to curtail his public appearances over time. Nonetheless, he and de Beauvoir unsuccessfully tried to launch a French television series summarizing the 20th century. He also moved from rampart to rampart, giving speeches, signing manifestoes, or making public appearances in support of some leftist causes, including the imprisonment of Andreas Baader by German authorities.

The Last Days of Jean-Paul Sartre

Sartre's physical decline began early, when he was 65. He and Simone de Beauvoir fought together the 10-year struggle against his blindness and illness. But being a truant child that he was, he would often slip her anxious surveillance and seem to be running towards the death. He smoked heavily and persuaded his numerous young girl friends to smuggle him bottles of Scotch and vodka. He would often be seen lying blind drunk on the carpet. "*I wanted to help you die cheerfully – I thought that was what you wanted,*" said an unrepentant woman friend who had spent an evening drinking an entire bottle of whisky with Sartre.

Simone de Beauvoir, whose semi-detached love affair and intellectual companionship with Sartre lasted all their adult lives, has told the story of his last 10 years in an emotional memoir, "*La cérémonie des adieux*" – The Farewell Ceremony. As time passed, his condition worsened as he became gravely ill. Strokes, diabetes, abscessed teeth followed by arteritis, uremia, and almost complete blindness. He lost control of his bladder and bowels, and his mind became erratic. He would report on imaginary visitors, see his cigarettes burning up in the gutter, and began to appear "rather sleepy, almost glum, with a fixed smile of universal kindness on his lips -- a smile caused by a slight paralysis of the facial muscles. But, " ... *he had absolutely no desire to die*," de Beauvoir tells in her book narrating with precision the detailed account of the last days of Sartre.

Almost blind, walking with difficulty, filled by the doctors with drugs to hold up his arteries – Sartre still wants the stuff of life. He mourns for his eyes but cares very little about loss of command further down. "*Some cats have peed on me*," he remarks mildly on a walk-through Rome. The pitying Simone, however, understands it all.

On the bad days, Sartre thinks his time is up: "*I can't work anymore . . . I'm gaga, as they say.*" Or, "*I'm not stupid. But I'm empty.*" But on the good days he looks for another 20 years or figures he has at least until the age of 81. "*All right*," he says to the film maker Michel Contat [139], "*I've done what I had to do.... I've*

139 "*Sartre par Lui-Meme*" ('Sartre by himself'), a documentary film on Sartre in French with English subtitles), was directed by Alexandre Astruc and Michel Contat. It was photographed mostly in 1972, but completed in 1976. In this documentary, Sartre openly said that the contradictions within himself were never satisfactorily resolved, especially

written, I've lived; there's nothing to regret. . .. I don't have the feeling of old age."

But his mental state is one of denial, confusion, and contradiction. While he says that "*there are not many things left that excite me" and that "I set myself on a rather higher plane,*" the behaviour reported by de Beauvoir suggests otherwise.

At the end, money was also a grave worry for Sartre. He had over-spent his considerable fortune as an author on needy friends and the causes he espoused. Earlier in an essay titled "*Self-Portrait at 70*, included in "*Life Situations*," a collection of his essays that was published in translation in the United States in the same year, he had written amusingly of his careless way with money, his fondness for music and the changes he had to make in his life when he could no longer see to read. And not only financial problem, to complete his larger works also, particularly the one on the French novelist Gustave Flaubert, "The Family Idiot", he had cut out all rest and relaxation and filled himself with stimulants. He, it seems, had consciously accepted a bargain: to produce his philosophical writings and die a little earlier.

"*Sartre had the decline and death his life demanded,*" de Beauvoir writes in her book. "*And that is perhaps why he accepted them so calmly.*" [140]

Death

On March 20, Mr. Sartre was admitted to Broussais Hospital, where he died on 15 April, 1980 evening from pulmonary oedema

---

the contradiction of being an intellectual as well as an activist. He speaks with special eloquence about the time of the German occupation of France, his frequently bitter, off-again, on-again relations with the Communist Party, and his increasing identification with France's New Left movement after May 1968.

[140] Smyth, Robin: "*Decline and fall of Jean-Paul Sartre*", From the Observer archive, 6 December 1981, Guardian, Retrieved on 2 December, 2012.

of the lung. His beloved de Beauvoir was by his side at the time of his death.

Describing the moments following his death, *Carole Seymour-Jones, in her book "A Dangerous Liaison: Simone de Beauvoir and Jean-Paul Sartre"*, writes: [141]

> *"Beauvoir had already taken a considerable quantity of valium and whisky and wished to be left alone with him. She sobbed at Sartre's bedside until early next morning. She attempted to lie beside him under the sheet, but a nurse prevented her due to Sartre's gangrenous bedsores. Beauvoir then lay on top of the sheet next to Sartre until five in the morning when hospital staff came to take him away."*

During his last years, in spite of his failing health, Sartre continued to speak out on political and social issues. In 1977, opposing the emerging trend of Eurocommunism independent of the Soviet Union, he accused the Italian Communist Party of collaborating with the Christian Democratic Party in a program of patronage and repression.

Until the end, Sartre remained an angry man and never minced his words. During his last days, even while commenting on his own country France, he wrote:

> "*As far as the state of French politics goes, I don't see a lot I can do, It's so rotten what's happening in France now! And there's no hope in the immediate future; no party offers any hope at all.*"

141 Seymour-Jones, Carole: "*A Dangerous Liaison: A Revalatory New Biography of Simone De Beauvoir and Jean-Paul Sartre*" Harry N. Abrams, 7 December, 2010.

Sartre never allowed death to bother himself. Fear of death hardly ever could change the way he lived. Till the end he lived true to his words he had written earlier in a book of photographs in 1978:

> "*I think of death only with tranquillity, as an end. I refuse to let death hamper life. Death must enter life only to define it.*" [142]

Last Words

"I love you very much, my dear Castor"

Sartre was on death bed.

Blood circulation problem had damaged his legs, arms, heart, eyes and brain. Since 20th March, 1980, his respiratory system began to suffer severe circulation problems too. He had developed pulmonary oedema and, therefore, not enough oxygen was getting into his blood. His blood circulation had also become so poor that his kidneys began to fail and his bed sores turned gangrenous.

On 14th April, 1980, when he was given a glass of water, he tried to look cheerful: "*The next time we have a drink together, it'll be at my place and it'll be whisky*!" Simonede Beauvoir, philosopher, author of "The Second Sex", icon of the modern feminism and Sartre's life time partner, was by his side. According to her, the following day, Sartre, no longer trying to be cheerful, asked her how they would pay for his funeral. Thereafter, drifting in and out of consciousness, he took de Beauvoir's (nicknamed "Castor") wrist and said:

"*I love you very much, my dear Castor*"
These were his last words.

---

[142] Whitman, Alden:" *Jean-Paul Sartre, 74, Dies in Paris*", New York Times, April 16, 1980.

Funeral

Paris "demonstrates against Sartre's death"

Sartre had not wanted to be buried at Père-Lachaise Cemetery between his mother and stepfather, so it was arranged that he be buried at Montparnasse Cemetery.

At his funeral which was held four days after his death, on Saturday, the 19th April,, there was an outpouring of grief more usually associated with actors than with philosophers. Film stars and politicians jostled with students, journalists, film-makers, social activists, folksingers, cafe philosophers and thousands of adoring young girls.

More than 50,000 Parisians descended onto *boulevard du Montparnasse* to accompany Sartre's cortege to the cemetery, as aptly said by a fan present on the occasion, to "*demonstrate against Sartre's death*".

Sartre's funeral procession

Years later, in a May 18, 2000 article for '*The Nation*', Daniel Singer rightly posits that such a demonstration of support for Sartre was:

"the last demo of the New Left. It was posthumous in another sense. The engagement associated with Sartre, the intellectual's or writer's social and political commitment, had been cast aside five years earlier by the self-appointed "new philosophers", crude in thought but skilled in propaganda, who loudly proclaimed that any attempt to alter society radically was bound to end with the gulag."

In this backdrop, Singer argues, Sartre's funeral procession is indicative of Sartre's numerous supporters, those who would rather have been "*wrong with Sartre than to be right with Raymond Aron*", Sartre's contemporary philosopher. [143]

The funeral started at "*the hospital at 2:00 p.m., then filed through the fourteenth arrondissement, past all Sartre's haunts, and entered the cemetery through the gate on the Boulevard Edgar Quinet*". Sartre was initially buried in a temporary grave to the left of the cemetery gate. Four days later the body was disinterred for cremation at *Père-Lachaise* Cemetery, and his ashes were reburied at the permanent site in Montparnasse Cemetery, to the right of the cemetery gate. [144]

According to a report written by *Agence France Presse* on April 19, 1980:

"Under a grey and leaded sky, in a meditation that no notable incident broke, thousands of people accompanied the mortal remains of Jean-Paul Sartre from the Broussais hospital, where he rested since his death, until Montparnasse cemetery. By its spontaneity, by the simplicity of the homage rendered, by the resigned silence, the crowd

---

[143] Dobrinska, Leah: "*Five Interesting Facts about Jean-Paul Sartre*", blogs librorum, A blog about books. Rare Books, Books Tell You Why.com. Jun 21, 2016.

[144] Cohen-Solal, Annie,: "*Sartre: A Life*", Translated by Anna Cancogni, New York: Pantheon Books, 1987.

gave to this ceremony the spirit that the loved ones of the disappeared wanted: no pomp, each coming "in their personal capacity". In that assembly of thousands of people, yet the friends were there, the actors François Périer, Delphine Seyrig, Yves Montand and Simone Signoret, Mouloudji, Léo Ferré. y difficult to distinguish the personalities and celebrities from other faces. The teams of "Liberation", "The Review of Modern Times" and Gallimard editions had decorated the coffin with flowers. Many authors were present: Claude Mauriac, Michel Foucault, André Glucksman, Françoise Sagan and several others

Just behind the head van came a car with Simone de Beauvoir, Sartre's companion and Arlette El-Kaim, the adopted daughter of the writer-philosopher.

After Sartre's death in 1980, de Beauvoir published his letters to her with edits to spare the feelings of people in their circle who were still alive. After de Beauvoir's death, Sartre's adopted daughter and literary heir Arlette Elkaïm did not allow many of Sartre's letters to be published in unedited form.

The exit from the hospital, at 2:00 p.m., by a narrow street, was hectic, hundreds of amateur photographers wanting, in addition to reporters, to fix the event. But very quickly, as the procession ended on the boulevard of the belt towards the Porte d'Orléans, young people made a chain around the cars to avoid jostling. Simone de Beauvoir thanked them with a smile.

The coffin was covered with roses, lilies and gladioli, and in the crowd people were carrying carnations, lilacs or daffodils in their hands.

From 2:45 p.m., on the outskirts of the Alésia district, the crowd was more and more massive, up to Denfert Rochereau where the famous "Lion of Belfort" was covered with people. More and more people came to overflow the procession and precede it as much as to follow it. The crowd was then from 15,000 to 20,000 people, according to various observers.

Children were perched on the shoulders of their parents, in small groups, young people discussing in a low voice the merits of Sartre, many participants held a copy of "Liberation" that Sartre helped to found, or sometimes a book of the philosopher.

At 3:35 pm the procession took the boulevard du Montparnasse, passing in front of "La Coupole", a meeting place for many Parisian intellectuals. We then joined the place du 18 juin opposite Montparnasse station. The streets narrowed. The procession passed in front of Sartre's home, at number 29, boulevard Edgar Quinet, without stopping. Jostling was already increasing.

Around 4:00 p.m., the procession arrived in front of the cemetery. There, both on Boulevard Quinet and in the middle of the tombs, a few thousand people were parked in peace. The mortuary van had a hard time crossing the front door of the cemetery.

Pushing back in front of the hood of clusters of curious people and photographers, the vehicle was walking along the aisle leading to the 18th division where the provisional vault of Sartre was located.

Everywhere, standing on the tombstones, trapped in the tiny alleys that run between the graves, perched on the roofs of the multiple chapels overlooking the vault, hundreds of people were trying to keep their balance. Jostling, shouting and even exchange of blows occurred when the hearse van (…) came to a stop in front of the pit.

It was very difficult for the funeral directors to extract the coffin from it and to lower it into the vault.

Simone de Beauvoir, a frail figure pressed on all sides and supported by her loved ones, mused for a moment. Upset, on the verge of fainting, she owed only to the muscular intervention of several young people, not to be crushed by the crowd. […] *she finally managed to get back to the car that was waiting for her at the end of the driveway.*

At the end of the afternoon, several hundred Parisians continued to parade, this time silently, in front of the tomb throwing red roses there and meditating."

Sartre was cremated the following week in *Père Lachaise* cemetery, then his remains buried in Montparnasse, in a vault located a few steps from his former home.

Six years later: Death of Simone de Beauvoir

Simone de Beauvoir died of pneumonia on 14 April, 1986 in Paris, six years after Sartre's demise, at the age of 78. Five years earlier, in 1981, she wrote her last book, *"Adieux: A Farewell to Sartre"* -- the only one written by her that Sartre had not read prior to publication. The closing lines in her book are as under: [145]

"His death does separate us. My death will not reunite us. That is how it is; it is already a beautiful thing that our lives were able to be in harmony for such a long time."

---

[145] Beauvoir, Simone De: "*Adieux: A Farewell to Sartre*", Bloomsbury Academic, 2016; p. 123.

"*Women, you owe her everything*!" So read the headline announcing de Beauvoir's death in April 1986. It was a phrase repeated over and over at her funeral, where some 5,000 mourners gathered to pay tribute to the writer many consider the greatest French woman of the 20th century, author of "*The Second Sex*", mother of the modern women's movement. de Beauvoir's ashes duly found their place next to those of Sartre, her partner in life, though never in marriage.

Epitaph

De Beauvoir wrote her epitaph for the tomb they would ultimately share. Taken from the closing lines of her last book, it reads:

"His death separates us; my death will not reunite us."

She is buried next to Sartre at the Montparnasse Cemetery in Paris.

The grave of Sartre and de Beauvoir in the Montparnasse Cemetery in Paris is often seen covered in lipstick kisses. Some admirers leave a more unique offering: "*Metro tickets*", mostly unused. It is said that a group of French Maoists that Sartre supported gave away free 'Metro tickets' during a fare hike in Paris in the 1960s.

Sartre's and de Beauvoir's grave in the *cimetière du Montparnasse* in 2016, with a new gravestone.

Chapter 27
Jean-Paul Sartre: Resurrection

He had died on 15 April, 1980.

Four days' later, his funeral on 19 April 1980 provoked an outpouring of grief more usually associated with actors than with an ugly, chain-smoking, foul-smelling, squint-eyed philosophers. More than 50,000 people took to the streets of Paris to follow his coffin and, as aptly said by one fan at the time, --- to "demonstrate" against his death.

But then, for the next two decades, his standing fell. His many mistakes and inconsistencies, his support for Stalinism in the early 1950s, for Maoism in the 1970s, his defence of civilian massacres in Algeria and at the 1972 Munich Olympics, obscured the range, versatility and ambition of his writing. [146]

So, it was not long before he passed into oblivion with new heroes of "post-structuralism", like, Jacques Derrida, Michel Foucault, Gilles Deleuze, Judith Butler etc. occupying the centre-stage in the intellectual world. And everyone thought Jean-Paul Sartre, the great French philosopher and the intellectual rockstar of the 20th century, had ultimately met with his end.

Foucault once dismissed Sartre testily as a man of the nineteenth century trying to think the twentieth. With his emphasis on consciousness, subjectivity, freedom, responsibility and the self, his commitment to Marxist categories and dialectical thinking, especially in the second part of his career, and his quasi Enlightenment humanism, Sartre seemed to personify everything

---

[146] "*The second coming of Sartre*", The Age, July 9, 2005.

that structuralists and poststructuralists like Foucault opposed. In effect, the enfant terrible of mid-century France had become the "traditionalist" of the following generation. A classic example of philosophical parricide.

Interestingly, Sartre's reputation as one of the most important thinkers and writers of the 20th century is rising again, not so much in France as "paradoxically" in high academic circles in the United States, a country he detested. The centenary celebration of his birth in 2005 has provoked a flood of re-examinations of Sartre's intellectual and political legacy.

Sartre's lifelong search for the meaning of freedom and his concept of institutional violence are now attractive to the black, female and radical academics in the US, who have formed the "*North American Sartre Society*". The young Americans see in Sartre one of the first people to pose the questions raised by the "*war on terrorism*", globalisation and the glib and often self-serving use of words, such as freedom and liberty by the dominant political and media culture of their own country.

Can freedom in the normal US sense have any meaning if it imposes misery on others, they ask. Is it not an act of bad faith if it is bought at the expense of global miseries, oppression of women and racial minorities?

Sartre dealt implicitly with issue of race in many of his works, beginning with *Being and Nothingness*. Race relations, especially segregation in the South, figured centrally in his reports [147] from the United States during his visit in early 1945 and were a major topic of his many writings on colonialism and neocolonialism thereafter. He was of the strong view that racism could not be separated from class, and that the black population must "*struggle*

---

[147] Sartre, Jean-Paul: "*Sartre on the American Working Class: Seven Articles in Combat from 6 to 30 June, 1945.*", Sartre Studies International, Vol. 6, Issue 1, 2000.

with white workers and on an equal footing with them for the recognition of their rights." Racism also formed the theme of his play, "*The Respectful Prostitute*" (1946), based on the 1931 Scottsboro trial of young black men in Alabama, who faced the death penalty on trumped-up charges of rape — some accused him of anti-Americanism for stressing the importance of racism in the United States. History has proved that Sartre was ahead of his time and definitely more perceptive than his critics.

In his writings, Sartre has claimed that even as a boy, whenever he heard of the French "*colonies*," he thought of racial exploitation. He wrote in *Black Orpheus* about the Africa poets using the colonizers' language against them in their poems of liberation: "*Black poetry in French is the only great revolutionary poetry of our time.*" He fulminated against the violence of colonialism and its implicit "*justification*" by appeal to the sub-humanity of the native population. On several occasions in diverse works Sartre referred to the cry of the oppressed and exploited: "*We too are humans*!" as the guiding ideal of their fight for liberty. His existential humanism grounded his critique of the capitalist and colonialist "*systems*." He wrote that "*the meanness is in the system*"—a claim that resonated with liberation movements then and now. His appeal for violence to counter the inherent violence of the colonial system in Algeria reached hyperbolic proportions in his prefatory essay to Franz Fanon's *The Wretched of the Earth* (1961). [148]

Of the other topics in current philosophical discussions, "*feminism*" is arguably the most important one to which Sartre offered relevant remarks,. This observation may raise some eyebrows because some of the images and language of his work were clearly sexist in character. And yet, Sartre always favoured the exploited and oppressed in any relationship and he encouraged his life-long partner, Simone de Beauvoir, to write *The Second Sex*,

---

148 "*Jean-Paul Sartre*", Stanford Encyclopedia of Philosophy Archive, April 22, 2004.

commonly recognized as the seminal work for the second-wave of the feminist movement. In addition to the plausible extrapolations of many remarks made apropos the exploitation of blacks, the Arabs, there are at least two concepts in Sartre's work that carry particular promise for feminist movement in the twenty-first century..

The first occurs in his short work "*Anti-Semite and Jew*" (1946) [149]. Many authors have mined this text for arguments critical of "*masculinist*" biases. The "*spirit of synthesis*" that Sartre champions here in contrast with the "*analytical spirit*" that he criticizes call for special attention. The issue is whether the Jew should be respected legally in his absolute Jewishness—his culture, his practices, including dietary and religious observances—or whether he should be satisfied with the "*Rights of Man and of the Citizen*" as his analytic, liberal democratic "*friend*" proposes. The abstract, analytic thinker counsels, in effect, "*You enjoy all the rights of a French Citizen, just don't be so Jewish.*" Sartre, on the other hand, argues for the rights of the Jew, the Arab or the woman (his examples) to vote as such in any election. In other words, their "*rights*" are concrete and not mere abstractions. One should not sacrifice the Jew (or the woman) to the "*man.*" In Michael Walzer's words: Sartre is promoting "*multiculturalism...avant la lettre.*"

The second concept that issues from Sartre's later writing which is of immediate relevance to feminist thought is that of positive reciprocity and its attendant notion of generosity. One is generally familiar with the conflictual nature of interpersonal relations in Sartre's vintage existentialist writings: "*Hell is other people*" and the like. But in his aesthetic writings and in the

---

[149] "*Anti-Semite and Jew ('Reflections on the Jewish Question')*" is an essay about antisemitism written by Jean-Paul Sartre shortly after the Liberation of Paris from German occupation in 1944. The first part of the essay, "The Portrait of the Antisemite", was published in December 1945 in *Les Temps modernes*. The full text was then published in 1946.

Notebooks for an Ethics, he describes the artist's work as a generous act, an invitation from one freedom to another. He even suggests that this might serve as a model for interpersonal relations in general. And in his major work in social ontology, *the Critique of Dialectical Reason*, Sartre charts the move from objectifying and alienating relationships to the positive reciprocity of the group members. Some feminist authors have employed these Sartrean concepts in their arguments. There remains much still to extract from Sartre's later works in this area in the days ahead.

Scott Mclemee, the "*Intellectual Affairs*" columnist for "*Inside Higher Ed", essayist and critic,* therefore, while chairing an academic symposium on Sartre in the US, rightly said:

> *"If Sartre's legacy once seemed a casualty of the Cold War, it grows ever more pertinent to the way we live now. The arguments over systemic violence, emancipatory struggle, and terrorism that dominated much of his work have now come back into view as matters of interest well beyond the community of Sartre scholars."*

Robert Stone, professor emeritus of philosophy at Long Island University, says that Sartre was committed *"to the idea that all freedom is interdependent, that if I am really to choose my own freedom, I must choose . . . a world in which basic needs are met, in which no one's freedom is subordinated to the systemic violence of dehumanising privation"*.

There are, however, discordant voices as well -- as there ought to be in an intellectual '*dialectic*' discourse. American writer Norman Mailer says that, to the contrary, Sartre gets you into dark and sinister territory. By attempting to prescribe a political ideal, without the compass of morality or religion, *"endemic nothingness installed upon eternal floorlessness",* Sartre leads you down a dangerous blind alley. [150]

Like it or not, Sartre is back on the stage.

----

[150] Swartz, David L. And Zolberg, Vera L.: "*Sartre for the twenty first century*?" Theory & Society, Vol. 36, No. 3, June, 2007, pp. 215-222.

Chapter 28
Epilogue

The "Other" Sartre - The Artist-Philosopher

When he was a very young man, Sartre said he wanted to be both Spinoza and Stendhal - in other words, to be a great philosopher and a great novelist or artist. Throughout his life, he alternated between political writing, and novel and theatrical writing. Ultimately, in his more modest moments, he seems to have regarded himself as a failure at both.

Despite the Sartre revival in the radical US, in the end it will probably be Sartre the artist-philosopher, rather than Sartre the political thinker, who would survive. The core of his thought - the concept of extreme truth to oneself, of constant personal revolution, of infidelity as the ultimate act of faith - is an artistic anarchist impulse, not a practical political one. [151]

Sartre's greatest creation was "Sartre" – a Picasso of 'written word'.

....

---

[151] Mclemee, Scott: "*Sartre Redux*", The Chronicle of Higher Education, November, 21, 2003.

References

1. Adler, Franz (1949). "*The Social Thought of Jean-Paul Sartre*". American Journal of Sociology, 55 (3): pp. 284–294.
2. Agence France-Presse: "*You are my destiny": Simone de Beauvoir's mad passion for young lover revealed in letters*", The Guardian, 22 January, 2018.
3. Alaigh, Arvin: " Black Skin, White ally: The complicated relationship of Jean -Paul Sartre and Frantz Fanon", https://africasacountry.com/2018/08/black-skin-white-ally]
4. Anderson, Brian C.: *"The Absolute Intellectual*" Hoover Institution, Policy Review, February 1, 2004.
5. André Gisselbrecht, Jean Roy, Jeanette Colombel, François Hincker, & Christine Glucksmann, "*Sartre est-il marxiste*?" La Nouvelle Critique. Revue du marxisme militant, March 1966.
6. Ang, J. M. (2019): "Can existentialists be happy? Authentic life, authentic happiness", Science, Religion and Culture, Vol. 6 No.1, pp. 122–129.
7. Appignanesi, Lisa: "*Did Simone de Beauvoir's open 'marriage' make her happy?*", The Guardian, 10 Jun 2005.
8. Aron, Raymond: *"Solzhenitsyn and European Leftism",* published in *Survey* 100/101, Summer/Autumn, 1976.
9. Aron, Raymond: *"The Opium of the Intellectuals",* Transaction Publishers, New Brunswick (USA) and London (UK), 2011.
10. Aronson, Ronald: "*Camus and Sartre: The Story of a Friendship and the Quarrel that Ended It*" (Chicago: University of Chicago Press, 2004), 128.
11. Baldwin, Thomas (1995). Ted Honderich (ed.). "*The Oxford Companion to Philosophy*", Oxford University Press. p. 792.

12. Bair, Deirdre: "*How Love Came to Simone de Beauvoir*", The New York Times", April 8, 1990.

13. Beauvoir, Simone De: "*Adieux: A Farewell to Sartre*", Bloomsbury Academic, 2016; p. 123.

14. Bakewell, Sarah: "*At the Existentialist Café: Freedom, Being, and Apricot Cocktails*", Chatto & Windus, March 3, 2016

15. Berk, Kiki: ""*"Hell Is Other People": Sartre on Personal Relationships*", 1000-Word Philosophy, 8 February, 2021.

16. Bernard-Henri, Lévy, "*Sartre: The Philosopher of the Twentieth Century*", trans. Andrew Brown (London: Polity,2003.

17. Betschart, Alfred: "*Sartre was not a Marxist*", Sartre Studies International Volume 25, Issue 2, 2019, pp. 77–91.

18. Bishop, Tom: "*Superstar of the Mind*", The New York Times, 7 June 1987.

19. Bondy, Francois:. "*Jean-Paul Sartre and Politics*". The Journal of Contemporary History. Vol. 2 No.2, April 1967, pp. 25–48.

20. Boyd, Brian: *"Vladimir Nabokov: The American Years",* Princeton University Press, Princeton, New Jersey, 1991, p. 138.

21. Brookfield, Thomas J. Riedlinger: "*Sartre's Rite of Passage*", The Journal of Transpersonal Psychology, Illinois, Vol.14. No.2, 1982.

22. Brown, Hannah: "*Simone de Beauvoir and Jean-Paul Sartre: An Existential Love Story*", Literary Ladies' Guide, An Archive Dedicated to Classic Women Authors and their work, July 26, 2018 | Updated December 3, 2020.

23. Butterfield, Elizabeth: "*Sartre and Posthumanist Humanism*", Frankfurt: Peter Lang, 2012.

24. Carole Seymour-Jones: "*A Dangerous Liaison: Simone de Beauvoir and Jean-Paul Sartre*", Random House 2011.

25. Cleary, Skye C.: "*Being and drunkenness: how to party like an existentialist*", Aeon.

Cohen-Solal, Annie,: "*Sartre: A Life*", Translated by Anna Cancogni. New York: Pantheon Books, 1987.

26. Cohen-Solal, Annie: "*Jean-Paul Sartre. A Life*", Translated by Anna Cancogni, New York: Pantheon Books, 1987.

27. Daigle, Christine: "*Sartre and Nietzsche: Brothers in arms*", Chapter 5 in 'Sartre's Second Century', edited by Benedict O'Donohoe and Roy Elveton, Cambridge Scholars Publishing, United Kingdom, 2009, pp. 56-72.

28. Davis, Lydia; Auster, Paul; Contat, Michel; Sartre, Jean-Paul: "*Sartre at Seventy: An Interview by Jean-Paul Sartre and Michel Contat*". The New York Review of Books, 7 August, 1975.

29. de-Capua, Yoav: "*The Great Betrayal: Jean-Paul Sartre and the Arabs*", Not Even Past, April 1, 2018.

30. Deirdre, Bair: *Simon de Beauvoir A Biography*", Simon &Schuster, 1991.

31. Deleuze, Gilles, "Desert Islands and Other Texts", 1953–1974, David Lapoujade (trans.), Los Angeles, CA: Semiotext(e), 2004.

32. Detmer, David: "*Sartre Explained: From Bad Faith to Authenticity",* Open Court Publishing Company, Chicago and La Salle, Illinois, p. 13, 2009.

33. Dobrinska, Leah: "*Five Interesting Facts about Jean-Paul Sartre*", blogs librorum, A blog about books. Rare Books, Books Tell You Why.com. Jun 21, 2016.

34. Farina, Gabriella (2014). "*Some reflections on the phenomenological method*", Archived 14 February 2019 at the Wayback Machine Dialogues in Philosophy, Mental and Neuro Sciences, 7(2): pp. 50–62.

35. Feinberg, Melissa: "*Curtain of Lies: The Battle over Truth in Stalinist Eastern Europe*", Oxford University Press, 2017.

36. Flynn, Thomas R.: "*The childhood of a genius*", Cambridge University Press, 2014, pp.3-4.

37. Flynn, Thomas, "*Sartre and Marxist Existentialism*", Chicago: University of Chicago Press 1984, p. 176.

38. Foucault, Michel, 1966 [1994], "L'homme est-il mort?" (interview with C. Bonnefoy), Arts et Loisirs, no. 38 (15–21 juin): 8–9. Reprinted in Dits et Écrits, Daniel Defert, François Ewald, & Jacques Lagrange (eds.), 540–544, Paris: Gallimard, 1994. 2001, Dits et Écrits, volume 1, Paris: Gallimard.

39. Fulford, Robert: "*The last words of a toxic intellectual*", The National Post, 22 September, 2007.

40. Gartzke, Erik; Rohner, Dominic (2011). "*The Political Economy of Imperialism, Decolonization and Development*". British Journal of Political Science. 41 (3), pp.525–556.

41. Gellman, Jerome: "*Jean-Paul Sartre: The Mystical Atheist*", European Journal for Philosophy of Religion 2 (2009), pp. 127–137.

42. Gerassi, John: "*Talking with Sartre: Conversations and Debates*". New Haven: Yale University Press, 2009, p.130.

43. George, Munduvel V.: "*Existentialism and its· Message to Indian Thought Pattern*", pp. 68-69.

44. Gloag, Oliver: "*Jean-Paul Sartre Took a Stand Against Empire*". Jacobin.

45. Hayman, Romald, "*Sartre: A Biography*", Da Capo Press, February 14, 1993..

46. Heidegger, Martin "*Basic Writings from 'Being and Time' (1927) to 'The Task of Thinking' (1964)*", Routledge & Kegan Paul, 1978.

47. Henley, Jon: "*Calls for legal child sex rebound on luminaries of May 68*", The Guardian. Retrieved February 23, 2001.
48. James, Clive: *"Jean-Paul Sartre"* in *"Cultural Amnesia: Necessary Memories from History and the Arts"*, W.W. Norton & Company, March, 2007.
49. *Jean-Paul Sartre*", Stanford Encyclopedia of Philosophy Archive, April 22, 2004.
50. Kunova, Marcel: "*Albert Camus and Jean-Paul Sartre: 'Lost' letter shows philosophers were dearest friends before their bitter falling-out*", Independent, 26 November 2014.
51. Krizman, Lawrence D. (Ed.): "*Sexual Morality and the Law*", Chapter 16 "Politics, Philosophy, Culture: Interviews and Other Writings 1977-1984, New York/London: 1990, Routledge, p. 275.
52. Lamblin, Bianca & Plovnick, Julie (Translator): "*A Disgraceful Affair: Simone de Beauvoir, Jean-Paul Sartre, and Bianca Lamblin*", Women's Life Writings from Around the World, Northeaster University Press, January 1, 1993.
53. Lawler, James: "*The Existentialist Marxism of Jean-Paul Sartre*" Amsterdam: B. R. Grüner, 1976.
54. Malinge, Yoann (2013). "*Does our past have a motivational effect? Our reasons for acting: Sartre's philosophy of action*". Vol. 4, no. 2. Ethics in Progress. pp. 46–53.
55. Malinge, Yoann (2016). "Sartre, "*The Transcendance of the Ego*"", The Literary Encyclopedia. Retrieved 25 May 2019 – via Academia.
56. Malinge, Yoann (2021). "*Sartre, "Existentialism is a humanism"*"". The Literary Encyclopedia. Retrieved 12 May 2021 – via Academia.

57. Marcuse, Herbert. "S*artre's Existentialism*". Printed in Studies in Critical Philosophy. Translated by Joris De Bres. London: NLB, 1972. p. 161.

58. McLellan, Joseph: "*Jean-Paul Sartre, Existential Author, Dramatist, Dies*", The Washington Post, 16 April, 2010.

59. Mclemee, Scott: "*Sartre Redux*", The Chronicle of Higher Education, November, 21, 2003.

60. Merida, Reda: "*On Jean-Paul Sartre and Palestine*", Middle East Eye, 20 May 2020.

61. Muscente, Kailee Kodama: "Categorical Imperatives and the Case for Deception: Part I", Teachers College, Columbia University, July 13, 2020.

62. Palau, Luis: "God Is Relevant: Finding Strength and Peace in Today's World", Multnomah, 1998.

63. Paul Sumit: "*Why did Jean-Paul Sartre turn a believer prior to his death*?", The Milli Gazette, 20 June, 2018.

64. Pejovi, Danilo, "*Jean-Paul Sartre*," Praxis: Revue philosophique, 1, 1 Zagreb, 1965, p. 85.

65. Poster, Mark: "*Existential Marxism in Post-war France: From Sartre to Althusse*", Princeton University Press, 1975.

66. Richard Howard: *"Sartre on the Nobel Prize – Jean-Paul Sartre",* (translated into English)), The New York Review of Books, 17 December, 1964.

67. Roberts, Glenys : "*Dangerous liaisons and sex with teens: The story of Satire and de Beauvoir as never told before",* MailOnline, 12 April 200

68. Sartre, Jean-Paul: "*Being and Nothingness*". London: Routledge, 1958, p.412.

69. Sartre, Jean-Paul: "*Tribute to Albert Camus*" published in "Camus: A Collection of Critical Essays" (ed.) by Jacqueline

Brian and Mary Danu sis Cooper, Germaine Bree, Englewood Cliffs, NJ: Prentice Hall, 1962.

70. Sartre, Jean-Paul: "*Nausea*", trans. Lloyd Alexander (New York: New Directions Publishing Company, 1964).
71. "*Sartre on the Nobel Prize*", 'Jean-Paul Sartre', Translated by Richard Howard, New York Reviewer, December, 1964.
72. Sartre, Jean-Paul, 1976. "*Sartre on Theater*". Michel Contat and Michel Rybalka (eds). London: Random House, 1976, p.199.
73. Sartre, Jean-Paul, 1976. "*Sartre on Theater*". Michel Contat and Michel Rybalka (eds). London: Random House, 1976, p.199-200.
74. Sartre, Jean-Paul: "*No Exit and Three Other Plays*", Vintage, New York, 1989, p.17.
75. Sartre, Jean-Paul: "*No Exit and Three Other Plays*", Vintage, New York, 1989, p.45.
76. Sartre, Jean-Paul: "*Notebooks for an Ethics*". Chicago: University of Chicago Press, 1992.
77. Sartre, Jean-Paul: "*Being and Nothingness*", Originally published 1943, Simon & Schuster; Reprint edition (1 August 1993), p. 246.
78. Sartre, Jean-Paul: "*Sartre on the American Working Class: Seven Articles in Combat from 6 to 24 June, 1945.*", Sartre Studies International, Vol. 6, Issue 1, 2000.
79. Sartre, Jean-Paul. "*Existentialism Is a Humanism*". New Haven: Yale University Press, 2007.
80. Sartre, Jean-Paul: "*Between Existentialism and Marxism*": Set 3 (Radical Thinkers), Translated by John Mathews, Verso Books, 17 January 2008.
81. "*Sartre and his Kafkaesque Nobel Prize moment, 1964*", Belle Meade Books, October 22, 2010.

82. "*Sartre on Death in Being and Nothingness*", that-which: Philosophy | Philosophemes | Philosophers.

83. Sartre and Rybalka, "*The Interview*", p.20.

84. Schaff, Adam, "*Marx oder Sartre*?", VEB Deutscher Verlag der Wissenschaften: Berlin 1965, p. 47.

85. Schuster, Shlomic C.: "*Revisiting 'Hope Now' with Benny Levy: A note on the 1996 English Edition*", Sartre Studies International 4, no. 1 (1998), pp. 63-75.

86. Schweickart, David: "*Sartre, Camus and a Marxism for the 21st Century*", Loyola University Chicago, Sartre Studies International, 24, 2: 24, 2018. Retrieved from Loyola eCommons, Philosophy: Faculty Publications and Other Works.

87. Seymour-Jones, Carole: "*A Dangerous Liaison: A Revalatory New Biography of Simone De Beauvoir and Jean-Paul Sartre*" Harry N. Abrams, 7 December, 2010.

88. Sherzai, Dilawar: "*Life begins on the other side of despair*", Daily Outlook, Afghanistan, September 04, 2014.

89. Smyth, Robin: "*Decline and fall of Jean-Paul Sartre*", From the Observer archive, 6 December 1981, Guardian, Retrieved on 2 December, 2012.

90. Stralen, Hans van: "C*hoices and Conflict: Essays on Literature and Existentialism",* P.I.E. - Peter Lang, Presses Interuniversitaires Europeennes, Brussels, 2005.

91. Strang, David: "*Global patterns of decolonisation, 1500–1987*", International Studies Quarterly (1991), pp. 429–454.

92. Swartz, David L. And Zolberg, Vera L.: "*Sartre for the twenty first century*?" Theory & Society, Vol. 36, No. 3, June, 2007, pp. 215-222

93. Temple, Emily: "*How Jean-Paul Sartre managed to spend his military service working on his novel* ", The Literary Hub, September 20, 2022.

94. "*The Drawings of Jean-Paul Sartre*", Open Culture, in Art, Letters, Philosophy, April 21, 2014.
95. "*The second coming of Sartre*", The Age, July 9, 2005.
96. Ursula K Le Guin: "*No Time to Spare: Thinking about what Matters",* Houghton Mifflin Harcourt, Boston, New York, 2017.
97. Wollheim, Richard. "*Freud*", London, Fontana Press, pp. 157–176.
98. Whitman, Alden: "*Jean-Paul Sartre, 74, Dies in Paris*", New York Times, April 16, 1980.
99. Zuraikat, Malek J. & Mashreqi, Sarah: "*The Death of God in Sartre's The Flies*", Acta Scientiarum. Language and Culture, vol. 42, No. 2, Universidade Estadual de Maringá, 2020.
